INTERNATIONAL PRIMARY ENGLISH

Progress Book 5

Student's Book

William Collins' dream of knowledge for all began with the publication of his first book in 1819.
A self-educated mill worker, he not only enriched millions of lives, but also founded a flourishing publishing house.
Today, staying true to this spirit, Collins books are packed with inspiration, innovation and practical expertise.
They place you at the centre of a world of possibility and give you exactly what you need to explore it.

Collins. Freedom to teach.

Published by Collins

An imprint of HarperCollins*Publishers*
The News Building, 1 London Bridge Street, London, SE1 9GF, UK

HarperCollins*Publishers*
Macken House, 39/40 Mayor Street Upper, Dublin 1, D01 C9W8, Ireland

Browse the complete Collins catalogue at
www.collins.co.uk

© HarperCollins*Publishers* Limited 2023

10 9 8 7 6 5 4 3 2 1

ISBN 978-0-00-865483-2

British Library Cataloguing-in-Publication Data
A catalogue record for this publication is available from the British Library.

Author: Daphne Paizee
Series editor: Daphne Paizee
Publisher: Elaine Higgleton
Product manager: Holly Woolnough
Content editor: Daniela Mora Chavarría
Project manager: Just Content Ltd
Copy editor: Tanya Solomons
Proofreader: Catherine Dakin
Cover designer: Gordon MacGilp
Cover illustration: Emma Chichester Clark
Typesetter: David Jimenez
Illustrator: Ann Paganuzzi
Production controller: Lyndsey Rogers
Printed and bound in Great Britain by Martins the Printers

With thanks to the following teachers for reviewing materials in proof and providing valuable feedback: Sylvie Meurein, Nilai International School; Gabriel Kehinde, Avi-Cenna International School; and with thanks to the following teachers who provided feedback during the early development stage: Najihah binti Roslan, Nilai International School.

MIX
Paper | Supporting responsible forestry
FSC™ C007454
FSC
www.fsc.org

This book contains FSC™ certified paper and other controlled sources to ensure responsible forest management.

For more information visit: www.harpercollins.co.uk/green

The publishers gratefully acknowledge the permission granted to reproduce the copyright material in this book. Every effort has been made to trace copyright holders and to obtain their permission for the use of copyright material. The publishers will gladly receive any information enabling them to rectify any error or omission at the fi rst opportunity.

Cambridge International copyright material in this publication is reproduced under licence and remains the intellectual property of Cambridge Assessment International Education

This text has not been through the Cambridge International endorsement process.

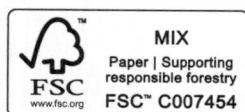

Contents

How to use this book

This book is full of questions. Each set of questions can be completed at the end of each week.

The questions allow you to practise the things you've learned. They will help you understand topics that you might need more practice of. They will also show you the topics that you are most confident with. Your teacher can use your answers to give you feedback and support.

At the end of each set of questions, there is a space to put the date that you completed it. There is also a blank box. Your teacher might use it to:

- sign, when they have marked your answers

- write a short comment on your work.

Date: _____

Now look at and think about each of the *I can* statements.

Pages 5 to 11 include a list of *I can* statements. Once you have finished each set of questions, turn to the *I can* statements. Think about each statement: how easy or hard did you find the topic? For each statement, colour in the face that is closest to how you feel:

☺ I can do this   😐 I'm getting there   ☹ I need some help.

There are three longer termly tests in the book. These can be completed after each block of units.

Answers and audio files for each test are available by request from www.collins.co.uk/internationalresources.

I can statements

At the end of each unit, think about each of the *I can* statements and how easy or hard you find the topic. For each statement, colour in the face that is closest to how you feel.

Unit 1	Date:		
Week 1			
I can infer meaning about characters in a story.	☺	😐	☹
I can answer questions about realistic fiction.	☺	😐	☹
I can identify types of nouns.	☺	😐	☹
I can use plural forms and *fewer/less* correctly.	☺	😐	☹
Week 2			
I can explain the meaning of some idiomatic phrases.	☺	😐	☹
I can find the main idea in a paragraph.	☺	😐	☹
I can read a paragraph aloud fluently.	☺	😐	☹
I can punctuate direct speech.	☺	😐	☹
Week 3			
I can find collective nouns in a puzzle.	☺	😐	☹
I can extract information from a non-fiction text and an epic poem.	☺	😐	☹
I can recognise a viewpoint and use it in writing.	☺	😐	☹
Unit 2	Date:		
Week 1			
I can read and understand persuasive language in advertisements and brochures.	☺	😐	☹

I can distinguish facts and opinions.	😊	😐	☹️
I can make notes about persuasive texts.	😊	😐	☹️
Week 2			
I can listen to, discuss and reflect on a story.	😊	😐	☹️
I can scan a text to answer questions.	😊	😐	☹️
I can identify words that are not Standard English	😊	😐	☹️
Week 3			
I can read a poem aloud with expression.	😊	😐	☹️
I can use pronouns.	😊	😐	☹️
I can follow a process to write a short persuasive text.	😊	😐	☹️
Unit 3	**Date:**		
Week 1			
I can predict the end of a folktale.	😊	😐	☹️
I can explain some proverbs.	😊	😐	☹️
I can use different adverbs in sentences.	😊	😐	☹️
I can read a folktale aloud.	😊	😐	☹️
Week 2			
I can read a text aloud.	😊	😐	☹️
I can identify parts of speech and give synonyms.	😊	😐	☹️
I can write a summary of a story.	😊	😐	☹️

Week 3			
I can spell adverbs with suffixes.	😊	😐	☹
I can form adverbs.	😊	😐	☹
I can scan a text for information.	😊	😐	☹
I can compare fiction texts.	😊	😐	☹
Term 1 Test			
I can read a poem and answer questions about it.	😊	😐	☹
I can recite a poem.	😊	😐	☹
I can write a persuasive paragraph.	😊	😐	☹
Unit 4	**Date:**		
Week 1			
I can read an extract from a classic and answer questions about it.	😊	😐	☹
I can make sentences with homonyms.	😊	😐	☹
I can write a short biographical text.	😊	😐	☹
Week 2			
I can read an extract from a play and answer questions about it.	😊	😐	☹
I can help to write a short scene from a play and then organise and perform it.	😊	😐	☹
I can take part in a discussion and evaluation of our performance.	😊	😐	☹
Week 3			
I can recognise and use direct and reported speech.	😊	😐	☹
I can write comments about a favourite character in a film.	😊	😐	☹

I can role-play an interview with a character.	☺	😐	☹
I can present a poem.	☺	😐	☹
Unit 5	**Date:**		
Week 1			
I can break words into syllables in order to read and spell correctly.	☺	😐	☹
I can identify arguments in a debate.	☺	😐	☹
I can write a letter to the press, presenting an argument.	☺	😐	☹
Week 2			
I can write simple and compound sentences with the correct punctuation.	☺	😐	☹
I can write a film review.	☺	😐	☹
Week 3			
I can read an extract from a story and answer questions about it.	☺	😐	☹
I can read a poem aloud and talk about it.	☺	😐	☹
I can compare poems.	☺	😐	☹
Unit 6	**Date:**		
Week 1			
I can use suffixes to make new words.	☺	😐	☹
I can explain what common expressions mean.	☺	😐	☹
I can infer meaning from a text and support this with quotes from the text.	☺	😐	☹
Week 2			
I can identify clauses and connectives in sentences.	☺	😐	☹

I can write sentences with more than one clause.	😊	😐	😞
I can express an opinion about a text.	😊	😐	😞
Week 3			
I can talk about the features of a fable.	😊	😐	😞
I can write text for a comic story and direct speech for a a fable.	😊	😐	😞
I can write a fable and make a presentation about it.	😊	😐	😞
Term 2 Test			
I can read a story and answer questions about it.	😊	😐	😞
I can write a short myth with dialogue.	😊	😐	😞
I can tell a story.	😊	😐	😞
Unit 7	**Date:**		
Week 1			
I can make notes about the content and structure of a non-fiction text.	😊	😐	😞
I can write an email in the appropriate register.	😊	😐	😞
I can take part in a discussion.	😊	😐	😞
Week 2			
I can identify and write sentences with subordinate clauses.	😊	😐	😞
I can compile questions and conduct an interview.	😊	😐	😞
I can read and compare different types of texts.	😊	😐	😞
I can use synonyms and vocabulary about space.	😊	😐	😞

Week 3			
I can write and spell opposite words using prefixes.	☺	😐	☹
I can identify similes and metaphors in poems.	☺	😐	☹
I can read part of a poem aloud with expression.	☺	😐	☹
I can write a short poem with a simile or metaphor.	☺	😐	☹
Unit 8	**Date:**		
Week 1			
I can listen to a news broadcast, take notes and answer questions.	☺	😐	☹
I can use modal verbs.	☺	😐	☹
I can spell words with silent vowels.	☺	😐	☹
I can identify a personal recount.	☺	😐	☹
Week 2			
I can use apostrophes.	☺	😐	☹
I can write a report about an event.	☺	😐	☹
Week 3			
I can identify the features of a magazine article and read it aloud in an appropriate way.	☺	😐	☹
I can listen to and extract information from a news broadcast.	☺	😐	☹
I can write, deliver and evaluate a news presentation.	☺	😐	☹
Unit 9	**Date:**		
Week 1			
I can explore vocabulary from a text.	☺	😐	☹
I can explore the features of commentaries.	☺	😐	☹

I can read a commentary aloud.	☺ ☺ ☹
Week 2	
I can read and write a short biography.	☺ ☺ ☹
I can read an information text and use the vocabulary from in the text.	☺ ☺ ☹
I can describe the features of different information texts.	☺ ☺ ☹
Week 3	
I can read a diary entry and answer questions about it.	☺ ☺ ☹
I can write comparative and superlative forms of adjectives and adverbs.	☺ ☺ ☹
I can write about climate change.	☺ ☺ ☹
Term 3 Test	
I can read an information text.	☺ ☺ ☹
I can write an information text.	☺ ☺ ☹
I can make a short presentation.	☺ ☺ ☹

1 What is 'realistic fiction'? Tick four sentences that are true.

☐ A story with a setting that is believable.

☐ A story that is not true, but could be true.

☐ A story that does not have any dialogue.

☐ A story with characters that behave like people in real life.

☐ A story with events that could happen in real life.

2 Reread this extract from *Saffy's Angel*. Answer the questions that follow.

Indigo was crouched on the hearth rug sorting through the coal bucket. Pieces of coal lay all around. Sometimes he found lumps speckled with what he believed to be gold.

"Come and help me look for Saffron!" pleaded Saffron.

"Find the baby first," said Indigo.

Indigo did not like the baby to be left out of anything that was going on. This was because for a long time after she was born, it had seemed she would be left out of everything, for ever. She had very nearly eluded his pack. She had very nearly died. Now she was safe and easy to find, third row up at the end of the Pinks. Rose. Permanent Rose.

Rose was screaming because the health visitor had arrived to look at her. She had turned up unexpectedly from beyond the black, rainy windows, and picked up Rose with her strong, cold hands, and so Rose was screaming.

"Make Rose shut up!" shouted Saffron from her stool. "I'm trying to read!"

"Saffron reads anything now!" the children's mother told the health visitor, proudly.

"Very nice!" the health visitor replied, and Saffron looked pleased for a moment, but then stopped when the health visitor added that her twins had both been fluent readers at four years old, and had gone right through their junior school library by the age of six.

Saffron glanced across to Caddy, the eldest of the Casson children, to see if this could possibly be true. Caddy, aged thirteen, was absorbed in painting the soles of her hamster's feet, but she felt Saffron's unhappiness and gave her a quick comforting smile.

Since Rose's arrival the Casson family had heard an awful lot about the health visitor's multi-talented twins. They were in Caddy's class at school. There were a number of rude and true things Caddy might have said about them, but being Caddy, she kept them to herself. Her smile was enough.

Caddy appeared over and over on the colour chart, all along the top row. Cadmium lemon, Cadmium deep yellow, Cadmium scarlet and Cadmium gold.

No Saffron though.

"There isn't a Saffron," said Saffron after another long search. "I've looked, and there isn't! I've read it all, and there *isn't!*"

Nobody seemed to hear at first.

Indigo said, "Saffron's yellow."

"I *know* Saffron's yellow! I've looked under *all* the yellows," said Saffron loudly and belligerently, "and I've looked under *all* the oranges too, and there *isn't* a Saffron!"

Rose wailed louder, because she didn't want to be undressed. Her mother said, "Oh darling! Darling!" Indigo began hammering at likely-looking lumps of coal with the handle end of the poker. Caddy let the hamster walk across the table, and it made a delicate and beautiful pattern of rainbow-coloured footprints all over the health visitor's notes.

"Why isn't there a Saffron?" demanded Saffron. "There's all the others. What about me?"

Then the health visitor said the thing that changed Saffron's life. She looked up from unpicking something out of Rose's clenched fist, and said to the children's mother:

"Doesn't Saffron know?"

a   What was Indigo looking for?

_____

b   What is the baby's name?

_____

c Think about the character called Caddy in this extract.

    i Write two facts that you learn about Caddy in this extract.

_____

_____

    ii What can you infer about her character from this sentence: … *but she felt Saffron's unhappiness and gave her a quick comforting smile.*

_____

d Describe the health visitor in your own words.

_____

_____

e Find a line of dialogue that tells you something about Saffron's character.

    i Copy the dialogue here.

_____

    ii Explain what this dialogue implies about her character.

_____

f What did the health visitor say that changed Saffron's life?

_____

g Explain in your own words why Saffron's name is not on the colour chart in their home.

_____

_____

3 Write the nouns from the box into the correct columns. Add one of your own words to each column.

> unhappiness   Cassie   Rose   hamsters
> homework   library   love   coal

Proper nouns	Common nouns	Uncountable nouns	Abstract nouns
_____	_____	_____	_____
_____	_____	_____	_____
_____	_____	_____	_____

4 Circle the correct word to complete each sentence.

   a She spends (fewer/less) time reading than I do.

   b Have you finished your (homeworks/homework) yet?

   c We had (bread/breads) and jam for lunch.

   d This colour chart has (fewer/less) colours than the chart in the shop.

   e The (child/children) are playing with paint.

5 Correct the spelling mistake in each sentence.

   a Saffron was tuff and not afraid to speak up. <u>tough</u>

   b Caddy thaught that the Health Visitor's children were not
very nice. _____

   c Indigo took eigt pieces of coal out of the bucket. _____

   d Other children fell asleep to lullabys, but not
the Casson children. _____

   e Caddy painted the hamster's feet in different coloures. _____

   f Rose cried because she didn't want to take her cloths off. _____

6 Rewrite the sentences so that all the nouns are in the plural form.

   a He has many book on his shelf.

   _____

   b I am making soup with fish, bean, tomato and potato.

   _____

   c What are those box on the patio of these house?

   _____

   d Divide the biscuit into half so that we can share.

   _____

   _____

Look at and think about each of the *I can* statements.

Date: _____

1 Explain what the underlined expression in each sentence means.

a My sister <u>saw red</u> when she discovered that I had borrowed her paints.

_____

b <u>Out of the blue</u>, a horse ran across the road in front of us.

_____

c She was <u>feeling a bit blue</u>, so we went for a walk.

_____

d I began <u>to feel green</u> on the rough, choppy sea.

_____

2 Read the extract below. What is the main idea in each paragraph? Look for the topic sentences.

I should explain right off that my real name is Salamanca Tree Hiddle. Salamanca, my parents thought, was the name of the Indian tribe to which my great-great grandmother belonged. My parents were mistaken. The name of the tribe was Seneca, but since my parents did not discover their error until after I was born, and they were, by then, used to my name, it remained Salamanca.

My middle name, Tree, comes from your basic tree, a thing of such beauty to my mother that she made it part of my name. She wanted to be more specific and use Sugar Maple Tree, her very favourite, because Sugar Maple is part of her own name, but Salamanca Sugar Maple Tree Hiddle sounded a bit much.

My mother called me Salamanca, but after she left, only my grandparents Hiddle called me Salamanca (when they were not calling me Chickabiddy). To most other people, I was Sal, and to a few boys who thought they were especially amusing, I was Salamander.

Paragraph 1

_____

_____

Paragraph 2

_____

_____

Paragraph 3

_____

_____

3 Work in groups of three. Choose one paragraph from the extract in question 2 and practise reading it aloud to your group.

4 Choose a name that you like and find out more about the name.

   a Write notes under these headings.

     Name

     _____

     Language or country it comes from

     _____

     Meaning

     _____

     _____

   b Write a paragraph about the name you have chosen. Start with a topic sentence and add two or three supporting sentences.

     _____

     _____

     _____

     _____

     _____

5 Rewrite this story with the correct punctuation.

Amalia

my sister's name is amalia she can be so bossy one day we were driving in the car to Bilbao, which is in Spain we were sitting in the back

    stop singing so loudly, Indigo she instructed I'm trying to read

    you shouldn't read in the car I replied it's bad for your eyes

    how do you know? just be quiet she ordered

_____

_____

_____

_____

_____

_____

Look at and think about each of the _I can_ statements.

Date: _____

1 Read the clues about collective nouns. Then find and circle the missing nouns in the word search puzzle.

Clues

a a … of friends

b a … of bananas

c a … of flats

d a … of flies

e a … of birds

f a … ants

m	u	b	a	f	g	w	i
c	i	r	c	l	e	u	l
o	p	s	a	o	f	t	q
l	b	l	o	c	k	p	c
o	u	j	t	k	i	s	a
n	n	a	f	u	g	o	v
y	c	u	s	w	a	r	m
r	h	t	i	f	n	j	a

2 Read this text and answer the questions.

Origin and meaning of names	
Aamir	Arabic; 'prosperous', 'prince'
Bello	West African (Fulani); 'helper'
Dipa	Sanskrit; 'light', 'lamp'
Katherine	Ancient Greek; 'pure'
Sabri	Arabic; 'patient'
Yuki	Japanese; 'happiness', 'lucky' or 'snow'

a Is the text fiction or non-fiction? _____

b What is the purpose of the text? _____

c What key features are used to make the text easier and more interesting to read?

_____

d Which two names have similar origins?

_____   _____

e Where does the name Katherine come from? _____

f If parents wanted a child to be happy and have good luck in life, what name could they use?

_____

3 Read the first two stanzas below from the poem *The Song of Hiawatha* aloud with a partner.

Then the little Hiawatha
Learned of every bird its language,
Learned their names and all their secrets,
How they built their nests in Summer,
Where they hid themselves in Winter,
Talked with them whene'er he met them,
Called them "Hiawatha's Chickens."

Of all beasts he learned the language,
Learned their names and all their secrets,
How the beavers built their lodges,
Where the squirrels hid their acorns,
How the reindeer ran so swiftly,
Why the rabbit was so timid,
Talked with them whene'er he met them,
Called them "Hiawatha's Brothers".

Then Iagoo, the great boaster,
He the marvellous story-teller,
He the traveller and the talker,
He the friend of old Nokomis,
Made a bow for Hiawatha;
From a branch of ash he made it,
From an oak-bough made the arrows,
Tipped with flint, and winged with feathers,
And the cord he made of deer-skin.

Then he said to Hiawatha:
"Go, my son, into the forest,
Where the red deer herd together,
Kill for us a famous roebuck,
Kill for us a deer with antlers!"

Forth into the forest straightway
All alone walked Hiawatha
Proudly, with his bow and arrows;
And the birds sang round him, o'er him,
"Do not shoot us, Hiawatha!"
Sang the robin, the Opechee,
Sang the bluebird, the Owaissa,
"Do not shoot us, Hiawatha!"

a Discuss the rhythm of the poem.

- How is it created?
- Read the stanzas aloud again to demonstrate the rhythm.

b Now write your own description of the rhythm. Give examples.

_____

_____

_____

_____

4 Answer these questions about *The Song of Hiawatha*.

a What kind of poem is this? Describe it in your own words.

_____

b Hiawatha calls the birds and beasts 'Hiawatha's Chickens' and 'Hiawatha's Brothers'. What does this tell us about Hiawatha?

_____

c Write three things that Hiawatha learned about animals.

_____

_____

_____

d Find synonyms for these words in the first two stanzas of the poem.

i shy, fearful: _____

ii quickly: _____

e Read this word: *whene'er*

i Write it in full, without the apostrophe: _____

ii Which two words make up this word? _____

iii What does it mean? _____

f Explain what happens in the second half of the poem.

_____

_____

_____

5 Read the story *Amalia* on page 17 of this book.

a What is the setting of this story?

_____

b From whose viewpoint is it written?

_____

c What is the writer's view of Amalia?

_____

d Which two verbs does the writer use to emphasise their view of Amalia?

_____ _____

e Rewrite this scene, with the correct punctuation, from Amalia's viewpoint.

_____

_____

_____

_____

_____

_____

6 Complete these notes on the steps for writing a story. Write notes about three things you do at each step.

Step 1: Plan

- _____

- _____

- _____

Step 2: Write

- Use your notes.

- _____

- _____

- _____

Step 3: Evaluate and present

- Read the rough draft aloud.

- _____

- _____

- _____

Look at and think about each of the *I can* statements.

Date: _____

1 Skim the texts below quickly and write short answers to the questions.

a What is the purpose of each text?

_____

b What is different about the texts?

_____

c What kind of language does each text use?

_____

Advertisement 1

Advertisement 2

Mike's Bikes

Mountain bikes on sale for *one week only.*

Wide range of models and prices.

25% off

See our website for all the offers.

Don't miss this special sale!

Get on a bike. Be free! It's a thrilling experience.

Bikes for sale

Wide range at unbeatable prices.

Pop in from Mondays to Saturdays, 9:30–17:30

324 Main Road, Somerset

See you soon!

2 Now scan the texts to answer these questions.

a Find and underline all the adjectives.

b Why are these adjectives used?

_____

c Which text do you think is more convincing? Give a reason for your answer.

_____

_____

3 Read these lines from different texts. Tick two lines that are *not* facts.

☐ Showing at the Civic Theatre from 23 August.

☐ An enchanting and memorable show.

☐ 324 Main Road, Somerset

☐ Bikes for sale.

☐ The most delicious pizza you will ever eat!

☐ For further details, contact MsMontana@EmailAddress.

4 Use this spider diagram to make notes about the features of persuasive texts.

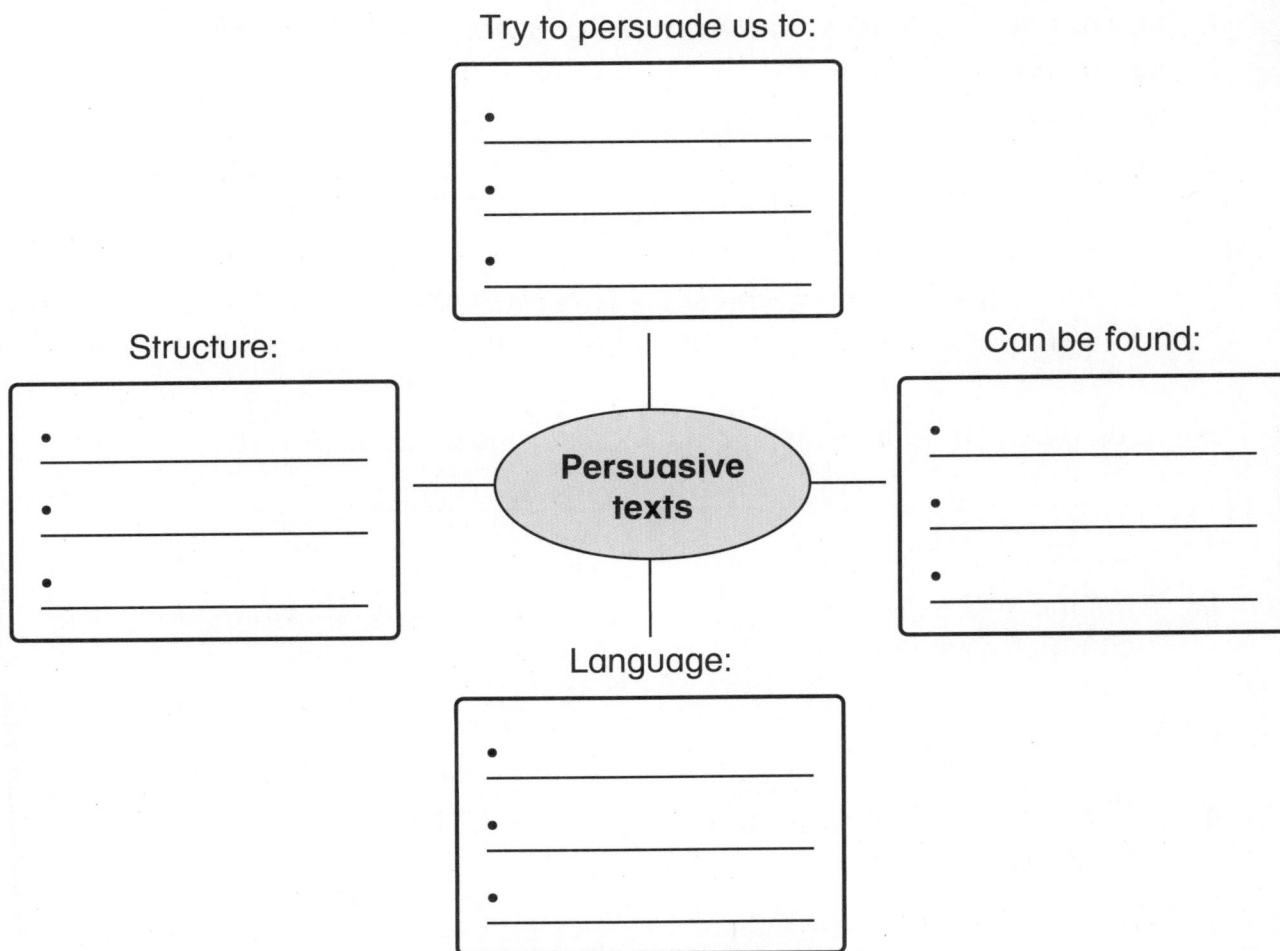

Try to persuade us to:

- _____
- _____
- _____

Structure:

- _____
- _____
- _____

Persuasive texts

Can be found:

- _____
- _____
- _____

Language:

- _____
- _____
- _____

Look at and think about each of the *I can* statements.

☐

Date: _____

1 **a** Complete the table about adjectives.

Adjective	Meaning	Opposite (antonym)
rigorous	_____	slapdash, superficial
_____	wonderful, amazing	dreadful, terrible, awful
spacious	_____	cramped, small
happy	_____	_____
_____	_____	ordinary
relaxed	calm, composed	_____
_____	tasty, scrumptious	_____

b Choose two adjectives from the table and write interesting sentences using them.

_____

_____

_____

2 🎧 Audio 1 Listen to the first part of the story *A Package for Mrs Jewls* again. Discuss the humour in this scene with a partner by answering the questions. Then write your own answers.

a Louis said "I'm Mrs Jewls". What was surprising about this?

_____

_____

b What did you expect the man from the truck to say or do when Louis said: "I changed my mind."

_____

_____

c The man says, "Here you go, Mrs Jewls" when he gives the package to Louis. Why is this funny?

_____

_____

3 Scan *A Package for Mrs Jewls* on page 22 of the Student's Book to answer these questions.

a Why did all the children raise their hands?

_____

b What does Mrs Jewls do to choose a student to open the door?

_____

c Why is Mrs Jewls's action funny?

_____

d Who opened the door for Louis?

_____

e Who said: "Get that piece of junk out of here" when they opened the package?

_____

f How does this reflect what the students thought about computers?

_____

g What did Mrs Jewls do at the end of the story that is shocking to the reader?

_____

4 Underline the words in each sentence from *A Package for Mrs Jewls* that are not in Standard English. Rewrite the sentences in Standard English.

a The school yard was a mess.

_____

b It wasn't his job to pick up the garbage.

_____

c He was just supposed to pass out balls during lunch and recess.

_____

d There was no elevator.

_____

e The truck honked its horn twice.

_____

Look at and think about each of the *I can* statements.

Date: _____

1 Choose the correct pronoun and write it in the space to complete each sentence.

a Mrs Jewls was teaching _____ about gravity. (they/them)

b There are two pairs of shoes. Which pair is _____? (your/yours)

c Don't make _____ angry. (her/hers)

d You look puzzled. Do _____ need some help? (you/your)

e Louis's face was pressed against the box. He couldn't see where _____ was going. (him/he)

2 Rewrite these paragraphs. Replace each underlined word with a pronoun.

a Louis held the package in <u>Louis's</u> arms. The package was heavy! <u>The package</u> was so big that Louis couldn't see where <u>Louis</u> was going.

_____

_____

_____

b Jenny, Jason, Allison and John took part in a spelling bee. <u>Jenny, Jason, Allison and John</u> had to spell words correctly.

"Allison," said Mrs Jewls, "the first word's for <u>Allison</u>."

John won the competition so <u>John</u> opened the door for Louis.

_____

_____

_____

_____

_____

_____

3 Look at the poem *Falling asleep in class*.

a What type of poem is this?

- [ ] an epic poem

- [ ] a narrative poem

- [ ] a limerick

Falling asleep in class

I fell asleep in class today,
as I was awfully bored.
I laid my head upon my desk
and closed my eyes and snored.

I woke to find a piece of paper
sticking to my face.
I'd slobbered on my textbooks,
and my hair was a disgrace.

My clothes were badly rumpled,
and my eyes were glazed and red.
My binder left a three-ring
indentation in my head.

I slept through class, and probably
I would have slept some more,
except my students woke me
as they headed out the door.

Kenn Nesbitt

b Name three of the features that tell you what kind of poem this is. For example: The poem is divided into verses (stanzas).

_____

_____

_____

c Why is this poem funny?

_____

d Read the poem to a partner. Use your voice as well as facial expressions and body language to make the poem interesting.

4 Write a short informative text of 2–3 paragraphs to persuade your class to do something. Include the following:

- a rhetorical question
- exaggeration
- repetition
- connectives
- emotive language

Write your draft here. Then improve it and read it aloud to your group or class.

_____

_____

_____

_____

_____

_____

_____

_____

_____

_____

_____

_____

Look at and think about each of the *I can* statements.

Date: _____

1 Read the following story and answer the questions.

Don't count your chickens …!

There was once a farmer called Dalmar. He grew groundnuts and cassava, which he sold at the local market. Year after year he had good harvests and his family were able to live very comfortably.

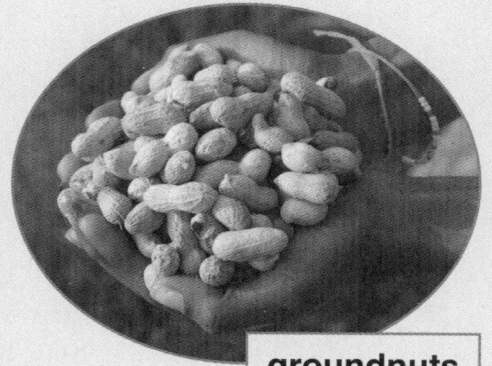

groundnuts

One year, Dalmar decided that he wanted to build a bigger house. He had saved up some money but it was not enough for his grand plans.

"I will use my savings to plant more crops," he said to his friends. "That way I will have bigger crops and make more money quickly."

Other farmers advised him not to do this. "There is a drought now and they say we will have floods next year," one said wisely. "Don't count your chickens …"

"… before they hatch," added another.

But Dalmar would not listen to the advice. He bought more seeds. Then he cut down trees on his farmland and prepared the ground to plant more seeds. He spent all his savings.

"We will soon be rich!" he boasted proudly.

cassava

a What type of story is this? How do you know?

_____

b Which crops did Dalmar grow?

_____ _____

c Find an adverb in the first paragraph that tells us about how Dalmar and his family lived.

_____

d Dalmar's friends said: "Don't count your chickens before they hatch." What does the proverb mean?

_____

e What do you think will happen next? Draw two pictures and add dialogue to each picture.

f Tell the story to a partner with the ending you have added.

2 Circle the adverb in each sentence and write what type of adverb it is (time, place, manner, degree).

   a She was very angry with me. _____

   b She went to sleep quickly. _____

   c I will cut these branches now. _____

   d Paul looked everywhere but he couldn't find his book. _____

3 Add adverbs of time, place, manner and degree to the sentences. Rewrite the sentences.

   a I will phone you. (time)

   _____

   b Shanti went without her bag. (place)

   _____

   c The mother closed the door so the noise didn't disturb the child. (manner)

   _____

   d They were pleased with the result of the match. (degree)

   _____

4 Circle the verbs in this paragraph. Then underline the adverbial phrases.

When she returned home she would light a fire in front of her hut.

One evening, she found that she had no wood. So she ran to the next hut and asked for a few sticks.

5 Proofread the following sentences. There are two grammatical errors in each sentence. Then rewrite the sentences correctly.

   a The storyteller is wearing a jacket long yesterday.

   _____

   b The woman chop some wood from the tree this early morning.

   _____

   c Everyone know the folktale about why women has long hair.

   _____

   d Them uses the wood to make fires to keep themselves warm.

   _____

6 Work in pairs. Take turns to discuss and read this extract from *Why Women have long hair*.

- Talk about how Bisi feels and acts in this part of the story.
- Then read the story aloud with as much expression as possible.

But one evening when it was time to make the fire, she found that she had no wood. So she ran to the next hut and asked for a few sticks, but her neighbour had none to spare and, in fact, though she asked in every hut nobody could give her wood to make a fire.

"Well," said Bisi, "I shall have to go to the forest and cut some wood myself because my son is away."

She took an axe and went into the forest, but she was very angry at having to waste so much time just when she should have been preparing the meal.

The first tree she cut down was the Iroko, which is a magic tree and must never be cut down.

"I don't care," thought Bisi. "I will cut off these low branches and chop them into sticks so that no one will know I have touched the magic tree."

In haste she did so, and soon returned to the village, carrying a large bundle of sticks with which she made a roaring fire and cooked a savoury stew for her supper.

Look at and think about each of the *I can* statements.

Date: _____

1   Work with a partner. Read the following part of the text about Rapunzel aloud. Make your reading as interesting as possible.

> **Rapunzel grew more beautiful by the day, and her hair grew longer and longer.**
>
> *Long golden tresses? That's more like it!*
>
> **And when the witch wanted to see her, she called, "Rapunzel let down your hair!"**
>
> *Bit rude, that, isn't it mate?*
>
> **"That I may climb the golden stair" and she climbed up her hair to visit her.**
>
> *Where's the prince? Isn't there a prince in this story?*
>
> **One day the king's son rode by the tower, and heard Rapunzel singing.**
>
> *So I was right then!*
>
> **And he fell in love and wanted to climb up the tower and see this beautiful girl.**
>
> *Don't stop now, what happens next?*
>
> **by Fiona Macgregor**

2   Explain the meaning of the underlined words from the text about Rapunzel.

a   long, golden <u>tresses</u>

_____

b   Rapunzel <u>let down</u> your hair.

_____

c   That I may climb the <u>golden stair</u>.

_____

d   Bit rude, that, isn't it <u>mate</u>?

_____

3 Find the following parts of speech in the extract about Rapunzel on the previous page.

    a a comparative adverb _____

    b a proper noun _____

    c a verb in the past tense _____

    d a common noun _____

    e an adverbial phrase _____

    f a personal pronoun _____

4 Give a synonym for each word.

    a dusk _____   **b** jealous _____

    c ornaments _____   **d** impolite _____

    e correct _____   **f** naughty _____

5 Write a short summary of the story of Rapunzel in your own words.

_____

_____

_____

_____

_____

_____

_____

_____

_____

_____

_____

_____

_____

_____

_____

_____

Look at and think about each of the *I can* statements.

Date: _____

1 Write these mispelled words correctly.

softir _____   highor _____

longr _____   carefuly _____

funilly _____   fearfuly _____

2 Make adverbs with the words in brackets and rewrite the sentences.

a Rapunzel did not cut her hair, so it grew (long) and (long).

_____

b She did (bad) than expected in the competition.

_____

c The one who climbs the most (careful) will win.

_____

d The witch attacked the king's son (fierce).

_____

e Rapunzel and the king's son lived (happy) ever after.

_____

f This time she sang more (beautiful) than ever before.

_____

3 Scan the text *Hairstyles* and find the following information.

Hairstyles

Hair can be cut, curled, straightened, coloured, extended or shaved right off. In Africa, hair braiding and hair cutting is an ancient tradition. If you want braids, the hairdresser ties long pieces of plaited hair into natural hair. Braids can be arranged in different styles, or have beads tied into them. Hairdressers can also arrange short hair into neat patterns, or cornrows.

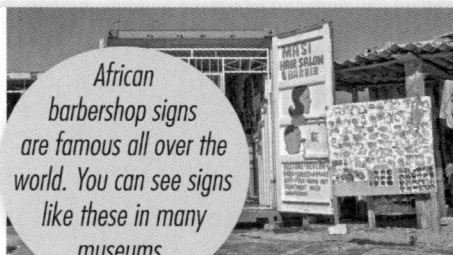

African barbershop signs are famous all over the world. You can see signs like these in many museums.

Braids can be used to create a number of different styles.

Dreadlocks are coils that form naturally in curly hair if it is not cut or brushed for a long time. People rub the hair between their hands to make the coils more matted.

a Two text features that show this is a non-fiction text.

_____

_____

b The name of a hairstyle that is made up of coils of curly hair.

_____

c Three verbs that describe ways in which hair can be styled.

_____

d The name of the hairstyle that is created with braids arranged in neat patterns.

_____

e The name of an African hair salon and barber.

_____

4 Use the table to compare what is similar and what is different about two fiction texts you have read this year.

Name of text		
Setting		
Main characters		
Type of story (for example: modern fiction, historical fiction, folktale, narrative poem)		
What the story is about		
Moral or lesson of the story		
Your opinion of the story		

5 Discuss the information in your table with a group. Share your ideas and opinions.

Look at and think about each of the *I can* statements.

Date: _____

1 Reading

Read the poem and answer the questions.

> **Extract from: 'A Bird Came Down The Walk'**
>
> **By Emily Dickinson**
>
> A Bird, came down the Walk –
> He did not know I saw –
> He bit an Angleworm in halves
> And ate the fellow, raw,
>
> And then, he drank a Dew
> From a convenient Grass –
> And then hopped sidewise to the Wall
> To let a Beetle pass –
>
> He glanced with rapid eyes
> That hurried all abroad –
> They looked like frightened Beads, I thought –
> He stirred his Velvet Head
>
> Like one in danger, Cautious,
> I offered him a Crumb,
> And he unrolled his feathers
> And rowed him softer Home –

a What type of poem is this?

_____

b Look at the first stanza.

   i What did the bird eat?

   _____

   ii Which words rhyme?

   _____

c Read the third stanza carefully.

   i What simile does the poet use? Write the two things that are compared.

   _____

   _____

   ii Which word has the same spelling pattern and pronunciation as 'bought'?

   _____

d What did the bird do when the poet offered it something to eat?

_____

e Which word describes the tone of this poem? **curious**   **furious**

_____

2 **Writing**

  a Find two pronouns in the poem, 'A Bird Came Down The Walk'.

   _____   _____

  b Write the plural forms of these words.

   eye: _____

   half: _____

  c In which verb tense is the poem written? Write two verbs from the poem to support your answer.

   _____

  d Underline the adjective in this line from the second stanza.

   From a convenient Grass –

  e Underline the adverb in this line.

   And then hopped sidewise to the Wall.

3   Writing

Write a short informative paragraph to persuade a friend to do something.

_____

_____

_____

_____

_____

_____

_____

_____

_____

_____

_____

_____

_____

_____

_____

_____

_____

_____

_____

_____

4   a   Read the following paragraph, which is muddled. Underline the two sentences that give main ideas.

My Mama, who is Polish, calls me Ama. My friends call me Mia or Lia. My first name is Amalia. Friends always seem to shorten names, don't they? The only person who uses my full name is my grandmother. Amalia is an old family name. My grandmother is also called Amalia. He says it means 'bossy'. Mama says she likes the sound of the name. My papa says that the name Amalia means 'brave' and 'full of hope' but my brother disagrees.

b Now rewrite the sentences in order as two paragraphs.

Paragraph 1:

_____

_____

_____

_____

_____

_____

Paragraph 2:

_____

_____

_____

_____

_____

_____

5 **Speaking**

Choose a short poem that you like. Copy it here. Make notes about how you will read it.

Which words will you emphasise?

What tone of voice will you use?

Then recite or read the poem aloud.

_____

_____

_____

_____

_____

_____

_____

Look at and think about each of the _I can_ statements.

Date: _____

1 Read this extract from *Alice in Wonderland* and answer the questions.

Eventually Alice noticed a glass table with a little golden key lying on it. Surely it must fit one of the doors? But she tried them all twice and it didn't. On the second time round she found a low curtain hiding a tiny door. The key turned and Alice peered through to the loveliest garden.

"Oh, I wish I could close up like a telescope!" she sighed. She wandered back to the glass table. It had a bottle standing on it. "That certainly wasn't there before," said Alice. The label said DRINK ME. It didn't say POISON or anything like that, so she drank it all.

Minutes later Alice had shrunk to about 25 centimetres high. "What a curious feeling!" she gasped. She'd become the perfect size for the little door, *but* … she'd forgotten the key. It was so far out of reach Alice burst into tears. As she did so, she saw a small glass box under the table with a tiny cake inside. On it were the words EAT ME, written in currants. Alice began …

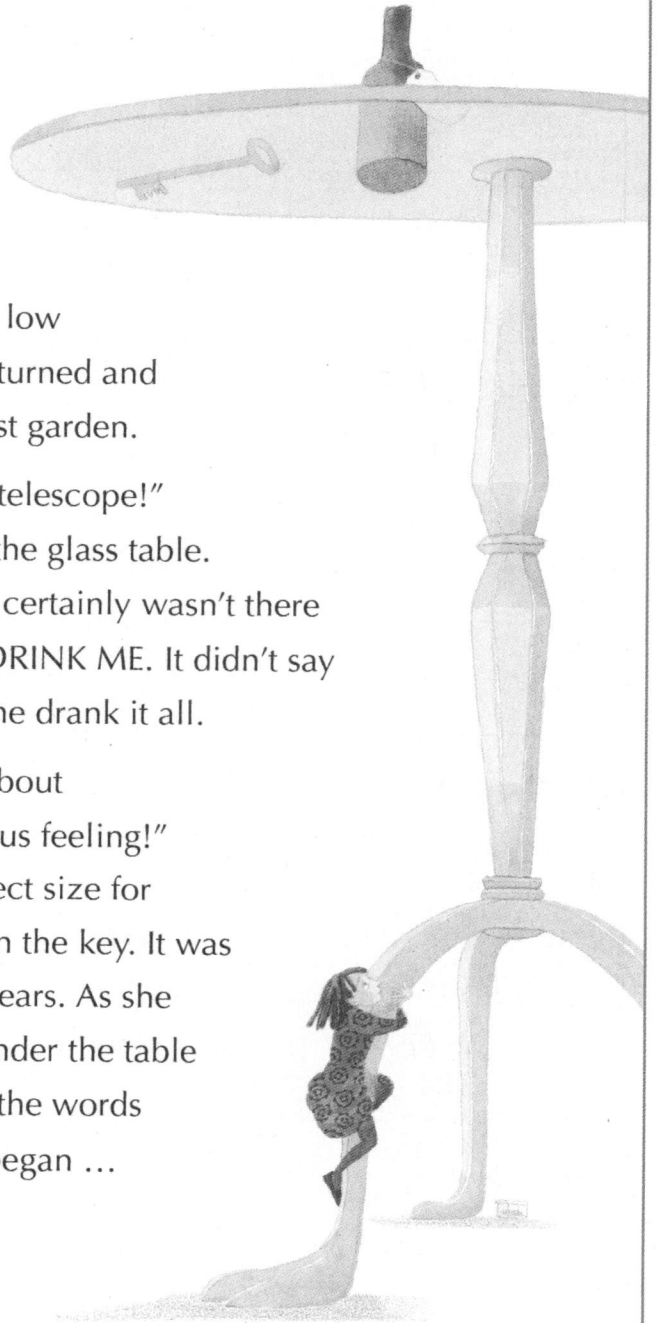

a What type of text is this?

_____

b What number would you look for if you wanted to find this book in a library? (Hint: Look in the Student's Book on page 41.)

_____

c Why did Alice wish that *she could close up like a telescope*?

_____

d Did her wish come true?

_____

e What do you think happened after Alice found the cake with EAT ME written on it?

_____

f What do these words in the text mean? Check the meaning in a dictionary.

peered: _____

currants: _____

g What do you learn about the character of Alice in this extract?

_____

2 For each bold word, circle the words that have the same sound at the end.

a **centre**   drama   popular   poet   character

b **coffee**   lazy   city   dry   quickly

3 Write two sentences using each word. In each sentence the word should have a different meaning.

Word	Meaning 1	Meaning 2
play		
scene		
cue		
band		

4 Read this biography of Lewis Carroll and answer these questions.

Birth name: Charles L Dodgson

Pen name: Lewis Carroll

Born: 27 January 1832 in Daresbury, England

Died: 14 January 1898 (aged 65) in Guildford, Surrey, England

Education: Rugby School, University of Oxford

Occupation: Writer, illustrator, poet, mathematician, photographer, teacher

Notable works: *Alice's Adventures in Wonderland, Through the Looking-Glass, The Hunting of the Snark, Jabberwocky*

Interesting information:

- Lewis Carroll had a bad stammer except when he was speaking to young children.

- He loved to entertain children with fantastic stories of dream worlds.

- He first told the story of *Alice's Adventures in Wonderland* (commonly shortened to *Alice in Wonderland*) to Alice Liddell and her two sisters while at a picnic. Alice told him to write the story down.

- The book *Alice's Adventures in Wonderland* was first published in 1865 and by the time Lewis Carroll died, it was one of the most popular books in the world.

a Where and when was Lewis Carroll born?

_____

b For which occupation do you think he is best known? Give a reason for your answer.

_____

c Make a list of three of his notable works.

_____

_____

_____

d Complete the sentence.

A _____ is a non-fiction account of the important dates and events in someone's life, written by someone else.

e Why has the writer of this biography used headings and bullet points?

_____

5 Write a paragraph about Lewis Carroll. The paragraph should have some biographical details and facts about the writer that you find interesting.

_____

_____

_____

_____

_____

6 Have a group discussion about Lewis Carroll and his work, based on the paragraph you wrote.

7 Do some research on another writer that you like. Make notes under these headings. Then tell your group about the writer.

Name: _____

Born: _____

Died: _____

Education: _____

Occupation: _____

Works: _____

_____

Interesting information:

- _____

- _____

- _____

- _____

Look at and think about each of the *I can* statements.

Date: _____

Unit 4 Reading a classic: *Alice in Wonderland*

1 Read this extract from *Who stole the tarts?* and answer the questions.

KING: Call the next witness!

RABBIT: Alice!

(COOK *leaves the stand.* ALICE *who has suddenly begun growing, jumps up and tips over the jury box.*)

ALICE: (*Apologetically*) Sorry.

(*Everyone in court makes a noise. The* JURORS *get back onto their seats and reorganise themselves while Alice takes the stand.*)

KING: Silence! Rule 42! All those more than a kilometre high must leave court!

ALICE: (*Indignantly*) I'm not a kilometre high!

KING: Let the jury consider the verdict!

QUEEN: No! No! Sentence first, verdict after!

ALICE: Rubbish!

QUEEN: (*Turning purple with rage.*) Hold your tongue!

ALICE: I won't!

QUEEN: (*Yelling at the top of her voice.*) Off with her head!

ALICE: Whatever. I'm not scared of you. You're just a pack of cards.

(*Pack of cards descends on* ALICE *while she tries to beat them off, half laughing, half crying.*)

a Where does this scene take place?

_____

b How do you know who the characters in this scene are?

_____

c Who or what is a 'witness'?

_____

d What does the expression 'hold your tongue' mean?

_____

e Underline two stage instructions that tell the actors how to act and speak lines.

f Explain why you think Alice is laughing and crying at the end of the scene.

_____

2   Work in groups of four. Write another short scene for the play *Who stole the tarts?* You can invent new characters or write what happens after this scene. Try to make your script entertaining. Your playscript should have the correct layout and punctuation, and include:

- a description of the scene

- the names of the characters

- stage instructions for the actors.

You can make some notes below. You can write your final scene in your notebook after you have edited and improved it.

_____

_____

_____

_____

_____

_____

_____

3   Discuss how you will act your scene. Then act your scene for another group or for your class. You do not have to use props and lights for this performance.

4   Use the checklist below to evaluate your performance. Discuss the performance with your group and then write your own evaluation.

Performance skills				
Acting: voice and body language	Excellent	Good	Some good ideas	Needs more practice
Stage management	Excellent	Good	A bit disorganised	Not quite there yet
Enjoyment	Excellent	Good	Some fun bits	A bit boring

Own evaluation:

_____

_____

Look at and think about each of the *I can* statements.

Date: _____

1 Tick three sentences below that are in direct speech.

☐ KING: Let the jury consider their verdict.

☐ "The queen is very mean," said Alice.

☐ The Mad Hatter said that he had sung to the Queen the previous day.

☐ Dennis said that he wanted to do the sound effects for the play.

☐ ALICE: They lied and said there was no room for me at the table.

2 Change the sentences below from direct speech to reported speech.

a "Take off your hat," the King told the Mad Hatter.

_____

b "I'm going to be a film star one day," said Ronda.

_____

c Jo said, "We will practise our play this afternoon."

_____

d Tony asked, "Can I play the role of the Mad Hatter?"

_____

e "I can help you write the words," Alice said to the Mad Hatter.

_____

f "What happened yesterday?" the interviewer asked Alice.

_____

3 Add speech marks and other punctuation marks to the sentences below. Fill the gaps with words from the box.

| explained | cried | inquired | complained |

a Did they invite you to join them for tea _____ the interviewer.

b No, they didn't _____ Alice

c It was a strange tea party _____ Alice to the interviewer. I didn't enjoy it.

d The Queen threatened to cut off my head _____ Alice

4 Write about your favourite character from a film you have seen. Explain why the character is your favourite.

_____

_____

_____

5 Work with a partner. Role-play an interview with Alice about the tea party. You can use some ideas from the interview on page 44 of this book, but use your own questions and answers.

Write your interview here in direct speech.

INTERVIEWER: _____

_____

ALICE: _____

_____

INTERVIEWER: _____

_____

ALICE: _____

_____

INTERVIEWER: _____

_____

ALICE: _____

_____

INTERVIEWER: _____

_____

ALICE: _____

_____

6 Choose any poem that you like that has at least two of these features:

rhyme   personification   assonance   alliteration   rhythm

Present the poem to a group. First, read it to the group and then say something about the features of the poem.

Look at and think about each of the *I can* statements.

Date: _____

1 Write these words to show their syllables.

witnessing _____   breakwater _____

phenomenon _____   horizon _____

triumphant _____   disturbance _____

2 Write these words in alphabetical order.

disturbance   describe   dotted   drawn   down   deer

_____

3 Look up these words in a thesaurus. Write two synonyms for each word.

a watch (verb) _____   _____

b phenomenon (noun) _____   _____

4 Read the following statements from a debate.

Decide whether each statement is arguing in favour of the debate or against it. Copy the statements into the correct columns in the table.

We can hurt the animals if we move them.

We should always try to save the lives of animals.

We may frighten the animals and cause the animals more stress.

A trained rescuer can save a stranded animal.

We only make their suffering worse.

Animals understand when people try to help them.

Should we try to help sea animals that are stranded on the beach?

Proposition (Argument in favour)	Opposition (Argument against)

5 You are going to write a letter to the press about attempts to save stranded animals. Follow these steps.

Step 1 Make a list of the features you need to use in a letter to the press.

- Express your point of view _____
- _____
- _____
- _____
- _____
- _____
- _____

Step 2 Plan your letter. What will you say in each paragraph? You can use some of the arguments from the table in question 4 or your own arguments.

Use this space for planning. You could use a mind map or bulleted lists.

Step 3 Write a draft of your letter in your notebook, using this template on the right to help you.

Step 4 Edit and improve your letter.

Step 5 Rewrite the letter neatly in your notebook.

Dear _____

_____

I believe that _____

_____

_____

_____

_____

Yours _____

Look at and think about each of the *I can* statements.

Date: _____

1 Write these sentences in Standard English by putting the words in the correct order and adding punctuation.

a near the beach at least a hundred whales there were

_____

b like crying I felt he said

_____

c coming and coming they kept the jogger told the gisborne herald

_____

d thought kahu's grandfather that a male the next 'whale rider' should become

_____

2 For each sentence, circle the verb and underline the subject.

a The jogger stared at the whales.

b All the people on the beach turned to look at the whales.

c Kahu loved the whales.

d Our whole family visited Wainui Beach last year.

3 Add a suitable subject to each sentence.

a _____ are huge mammals that live in the oceans.

b _____ liked to swim with the whales every day.

c _____ hired a helicopter to fly over the whales.

d _____ sent reporters and photographers to the scene.

4 Join the simple sentences to make compound sentences. Use suitable connectives.

  a The waves break over them. The waves hiss around their passive frames.

  _____

  _____

  b His lips were trembling. His eyes were moist with tears.

  _____

  _____

  c She likes to swim with the whales. Some people think this is dangerous.

  _____

  _____

  d Her father was furious. Her mother was not furious.

  _____

  _____

5 Write a short review of any film that you have watched recently.
    Use these headings:

Title: _____

Actors: _____

Director: _____

What the film is about:

_____

_____

Your opinion of the film:

_____

_____

Star rating: ☆ ☆ ☆ ☆ ☆

Why you recommend or don't recommend the film:

_____

_____

Look at and think about each of the *I can* statements.

Date: _____

1 Reread the extract from *The Whale Rider (Text 2)*. Answer the questions that follow.

Text 2

Nobody saw her slip away and enter the water. Nobody knew at all until she was half way through the waves. Then the headlights and spotlights from the cars along the beach picked up her white dress and that little head bobbing up and down in the waves. As soon as I saw her, I knew it was Kahu.

"Hey!" I yelled. I pointed through the driving rain. Other spotlights began to catch her. In that white dress and white beribboned pigtails, she was like a small puppy, trying to keep its head up. A wave would crash over her, but somehow she would appear on the other side, gasping wide-eyed, and doing what looked like a cross between a dog paddle and a breast stroke.

Instantly I ran through the waves. People said I acted like a maniac. I plunged into the sea.
If the whale lives, we live. These were the only words Kahu could think of.

We have lost our way of talking to whales.

The water was freezing, but not to worry. The waves were huge, but kei te pai. The rain was like spears, but hei aha.

Every now and then she had to take a deep breath because sometimes the waves were like dumpers, slamming her down to the sandy bottom, but somehow she bobbed right back up like a cork. Now the trouble was that the lights from the beach were dazzling her eyes, making it hard to see where she was going. Her neck was hurting with the constant looking up, but

there, there, was the whale with the moko. She dog paddled purposefully towards it. A wave smashed into her and she swallowed more seawater. She began to cough and tread water. Then she set her face with determination. As she approached the whale, she suddenly remembered what she was supposed to do.

"Karanga mai, karanga mai, karanga mai." She raised her head and began to call to the whale.

The headlights and spotlights were dazzling upon the whale. It may have been the sudden light, or a cross current, but the eye of the whale seemed to flicker. Then the whale appeared to be looking at the young girl swimming.

Ko Kahutia Te Rangi?

"Kahu!" I could hear Granny Flowers screaming in the wind.

My boots were dragging me down. I had to stop and reach under to take them off. I looked up. I tried to see where Kahu was. The waves lifted me up and down.

"Kahu, no!" I cried.

She had reached the whale and was hanging onto its jaw.

"Help me," she cried. "Ko Kahutia Te Rangi au. Ko Paikea."

The whale shuddered at the words.

By chance, Kahu felt the whale's forward fin. Her fingers tightened quickly around it. She held on for dear life.

And the whale felt a surge of gladness which, as it mounted, became ripples of ecstasy, ever increasing. He began to communicate his joy to all parts of his body.

Out beyond the breakwater the herd suddenly became alert. With hope rising, they began to sing their encouragement to their leader.

She was going, our Kahu. She was going into the deep ocean. I could hear her small piping voice in the darkness as she left us.

She was going with the whales into the sea and the rain. She was a small figure in a white dress, kicking the whale as if it was a horse, her braids swinging in the rain. Then she was gone and we were left behind.

Ko Paikea, ko Paikea.

a How did other people know that Kahu was in the water?

_____

b Describe the setting of this text.

_____

c Read these words: *Karangi mai*

   i What do the words mean? _____

   ii Who said the words? _____

   iii Why did the person repeat the words? _____

d What do the underlined words in this sentence mean? Tick (✓) one box.

She began to cough and <u>tread water</u>.

☐ swallow water   ☐ go under the water

☐ stay upright in water by moving the feet and hands

e What mood has the writer created in the first part of this extract? Circle two words in the box to describe the mood.

> foreboding   gloomy   tense   cheerful   peaceful

f Read this paragraph from the extract.

And the whale felt a surge of gladness which, as it mounted, became ripples of ecstasy, ever increasing. He began to communicate his joy to all parts of his body.

   i Which emotive words does the writer use here? Underline them.

   ii Has the mood changed? How? _____

   iii How do these words make you feel? _____

2 Read or sing the poem 'Sea Fever' aloud to a partner or in a group.

Sea Fever

I must go down to the seas again, to the lonely sea and the sky
And all I ask is a tall ship, and a star to steer her by;
And the wheel's kick and the wind's song and the white sail's shaking
And a grey mist on the sea's face, and a grey dawn breaking.

I must go down to the seas again, for the call of the running tide
Is a wild call and a clear call that may not be denied;
And all I ask is a windy day with the white clouds flying,
And the flung spray and the blown spume, and the sea-gulls crying.

I must go down to the seas again, to the vagrant gypsy life,
To the gull's way and the whale's way where the wind's like a whetted knife;
And all I ask is a merry yarn from a laughing fellow-rover,
And quiet sleep and a sweet dream when the long trick's over.

John Masefield

3   Write an example of each of these figures of speech from the poem 'Sea Fever'.

alliteration: _____

personification: _____

repetition: _____

simile: _____

rhyming words: _____

4   What type of poem is it? Describe the features of this type of poem to a partner.

5   Compare this poem with another poem that you have read. Use the table below to do this.

	Sea Fever	_____
Theme		
Type of poem		
Structure		
Rhythm		
Choice of words		

Look at and think about each of the *I can* statements.

Date: _____

1 Circle the prefixes in the words in the box and then complete the spelling rule.

> disappear   welcome   already   misspell   unlikely

Rule: When you use **well** or **all** as a prefix, drop _____. Otherwise, the prefixes stay the same.

2 What do you have to do to add suffixes to these words? Complete the spelling rules.

Word	Suffix	Spelling rule
manage	-ment	add the suffix, no changes
heavy	-ly	
deny	-ed	
empty	-ing	
hope	-fully	
marvel	-ing	
care	-ing	

3 Add a suffix to each word in brackets to make a word that is grammatically correct in the sentence.

a The friends had a _____ party. (love)

b Ben _____ Phoebe's presentation several times. (interrupt)

c Pandora looked _____ frightened. (extreme)

d Everyone was _____ at Phoebe. (stare)

e They gave her _____ things. (wonder)

f She opened the box _____ . (careful)

4 Write the meaning of the underlined expression in each sentence.

a She has <u>the Midas Touch</u>.

_____

b <u>Don't burn the candle at both ends</u>! You will get ill.

_____

c You need <u>to bury the hatchet</u> if you want to remain good friends.

_____

d Dan and Andi arrived <u>at the eleventh hour</u>!

_____

5 Read this extract from *Walk Two Moons*.

> "At this civilised dinner, Zeus asked the Olympians to give the beautiful woman presents – to make her feel like a welcome guest." Phoebe glanced at me. "They gave her all kinds of wonderful things: a fancy shawl, a silver dress, beauty—"
>
> Ben interrupted. "I thought you said she was already beautiful."
>
> "I know. They gave her *more* beauty. Are you satisfied?" Her lip was no longer trembling. Now she was blushing. "The Olympians also gave her the ability to sing, the power of persuasion, a gold crown, flowers and many truly wonderful things such as that. Because of all these gifts, Zeus named her Pandora, which means 'the gift of all'."
>
> Her heart attack was apparently subsiding. She was getting into it. "There were two other gifts that I have not mentioned yet. One of them was curiosity. That is why all women are curious, by the way, because it was a gift given to the very first woman."
>
> Ben said, "I wish she had been given the gift of silence."
>
> "As I was *saying*," Phoebe continued, "Pandora was given curiosity. There was one more gift, too, and that was a beautiful box, covered in gold and jewels, *but* – and this is very important – she was forbidden to open the box."

Find a quote from the story to support each of these statements.

a Ben doubted what Phoebe was saying about the woman.

_____

b Phoebe was embarrassed when Ben interrupted her.

_____

c Phoebe began to feel better and less nervous during the presentation.

_____

d Phoebe becomes irritated with the way Ben interrupts her presentation.

_____

6 Make a summary of the first three paragraphs from the story.

a Underline the main ideas.

b Cross out words like adjectives and adverbs.

c Write the main ideas in your own words here.

_____

_____

_____

Look at and think about each of the *I can* statements.

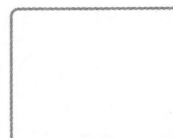

Date: _____

1 Underline the main clause in each sentence. Circle the connective.

a She always blushes when she is nervous.

b Mr Birkway scratched his head because he was puzzled.

c Phoebe was nervous before she made the presentation.

d Pandora opened the box because she was curious.

e Although I was nervous, I continued the presentation.

f I was bored listening to the story so I started to interrupt.

2 Add a subordinate clause to the main clause in each of these sentences.

a Ben interrupted because _____

_____

b Shigeru asked a question so _____

_____

c Phoebe hesitated because _____

_____

d The Olympians gave the woman gifts so _____

_____

e Although _____
I listened to the rest of the story.

f Because _____ all the evil things escaped.

3 Rewrite the sentences, correcting the mistakes.

a Phoebe she is blushing when she is nervous.

_____

b The students is making a presentation about myth.

_____

c After Zeus creating Pandora, he invite the Olympians to dinner.

_____

d Mr Birkway interrupt to help Pandora explains what 'hope' means.

_____

4 Make notes about the good gifts mentioned in the story you read in your Student Book on pages 66–67. You can add ideas of your own. You can use lists or a mind map.

[   ]

5 Write two paragraphs about the myth *Pandora's Box*.

Paragraph 1: Explain why it is a myth.

_____

_____

_____

Paragraph 2: State your opinion of the myth. Start with a main idea and then add supporting ideas.

_____

_____

_____

6 Discuss your opinions about the story with a group.

Look at and think about each of the *I can* statements.

Date: _____

1 Reread the story *Anansi and Horse*. Answer the questions that follow.

Anansi and Horse

One day Anansi asked Horse to go with him to cut plantains. When they had finished cutting the plantains, they carried them out to a clearing and began to play a game – stick, lick stick. After a while Anansi said, "Brer Horse, we are hungry now but we don't have a fire to roast the plantains. Do you see that fire up there on the hill? Please gallop up there and get a lighted stick so we can make a fire and roast the plantains." Horse immediately flung up his tail and galloped off.

As soon as the horse was gone, Anansi took out a tinderbox and built a big fire. He roasted all the plantains and then he quickly ate all but four of them.

When Horse came back, Anansi explained that a man had come by, and helped him to make a fire. Anansi had roasted the plantains so that he could share them with Horse. But then another man had come by, beaten Anansi and stolen all but the four leftover plantains. Brer Horse said, "Never mind. You take two and I'll take two." And Horse took his two quite happily.

Brer Goat had been hiding behind a bush and he'd seen what Anansi had done, so the next day, he called on Anansi to go and cut plantains with him. Goat and Anansi went out, cut plantains and carried them to the clearing. Anansi then said, "Brer Goat, we are hungry now, but we don't have a fire to roast the plantains. Do you see that fire up there on the hill? Please trot up there and get a lighted stick so we can make a fire and roast the plantains." Goat trotted off, but he ran round a clump of bushes and watched Anansi.

Anansi took out his tinderbox and made a fire. Once he'd peeled all the plantains and put them on the fire to roast, Goat jumped out of the bush and grabbed a stick. He lit the stick and set fire to the grass in a circle around the fire.

"Put your hand in there and steal the plantains, Sir," he said to Anansi. Goat then jumped neatly over the ring of fire, and began to gather up the nicely roasted plantains. Anansi begged and cried for his share, but Goat took them all and ran off.

Anansi was left with absolutely none.

a What type of story is this? Give a reason for your answer.

_____

b How did Anansi cook the plantains?

_____

c Why is Anansi usually described as a 'trickster character'? Support your answer with ideas from the story.

_____

d Explain how Brer Goat tricked Anansi.

_____

_____

_____

e What is the moral or lesson of this story?

_____

2 Look at the pictures, which show the conclusion of the story. Add words to the speech bubbles to show what each character says. Use your own words.

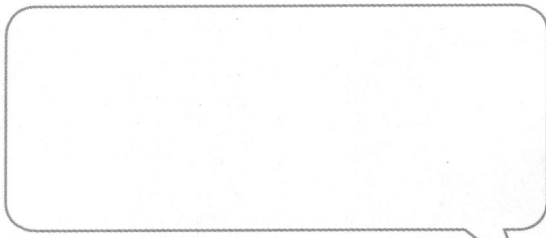

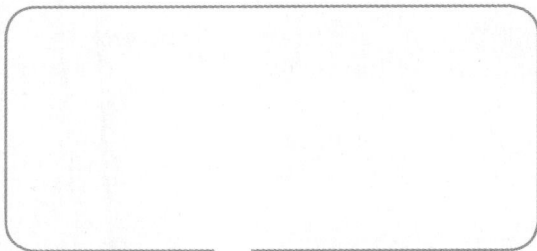

3 Use the pictures to retell this story about Anansi to a partner.

1

2

3

4

5

6

7

8

9

10

11

12

4   Work in pairs. Discuss the structure of the story about Anansi and Firefly. Make notes about the structure in the table below.

Stage	Event in story
Introduction	Firefly came to visit Anansi. They decided to go on an egg hunt.
Build-up	
Climax	
Resolution	
Conclusion	

5   Write your own fable using the structure of a good story. You can draw a table like the one above and use it to plan your story in your notebook.

6   Make a presentation of your story to the class.

Look at and think about each of the *I can* statements.

Date: _____

1 Reading

Read the story and then answer the questions.

The Southern Cross – Giraffe becomes a star

The Southern Cross is another constellation that has many stories about it.

The San peoples in South Africa tell the story of all the animals on Earth having a job to do, except for Giraffe.

Giraffe wanted to be useful like the other animals, so one day, the animals had a good idea. As the Sun often got lost on its journey across the sky, it needed someone to guide it.

Giraffe was so tall that he could poke his head above the trees and help the Sun.

Whenever the Sun went the wrong way, Giraffe stretched his long neck and nudged it back into place. To thank him, some of the stars moved so that they always pointed at the Sun. The local people called this constellation "Giraffe".

Fact File

Culture: San peoples

Place: Southern Africa

Did you know?

The Southern Cross is made mainly of four bright stars. Some people see the shape of a cross in the stars. Others see lions, trees, emus, or the **talons** of a giant eagle.

a What type of story is this?

_____

b What is the purpose of this story?

_____

c Where does the story come from?

_____

d What did giraffe offer to do?

_____

e How do other cultures explain the shape of this constellation?

_____

2 **Writing**

a Add a collective noun from the text to this sentence.

Orion is a _____ of stars.

b Give a synonym for this word from the story.

push _____

c Read the following sentence.

I also want a job complained Giraffe.

i Punctuate the sentence as direct speech.

_____

ii Write the sentence as reported speech.

_____

d Write the following sentences as a compound sentence.

Giraffe stretched its long neck.

Giraffe nudged the Sun back into place.

_____

_____

3   Writing

a   Write a short myth that you know well. You can also use the story of the Giraffe that you read.

Write the story as a myth. Your myth should have the following features:

- an opening sentence that tells us that it is a myth and where the myth comes from.

- plot with dialogue

- an ending that explains why the myth was told.

Use this space to plan your myth.

b Then draft, edit and improve it.

_____

_____

_____

_____

_____

_____

_____

_____

_____

_____

_____

_____

_____

_____

_____

_____

_____

_____

_____

_____

4 **Speaking**

Tell your myth to your group or class. Use gestures and body language to make the myth interesting to listen to.

Look at and think about each of the *I can* statements.

Date: _____

1 Read the text *How do astronauts live in space?*. Make notes about the text, using the headings below.

How do astronauts live in space?

The main difference between living in space and living on Earth is the floating problem! Here on Earth we have a force called gravity, which pulls us towards Earth, and gives us weight.

Gravity gets less and less as you move further from Earth, and if you get far enough away you become weightless and you float.

Astronauts eat food from sealed containers, and they put the empty packets into a special bin afterwards. They can't put salt and pepper on their food, because the salt and pepper floats away!

When astronauts need to sleep they tie themselves down, otherwise they could float around and bump into things. They usually sleep in sleeping bags.

Astronauts wear ordinary clothes, like tracksuits and T-shirts inside the spacecraft. They don't often wash or change their clothes. The clothes don't get dirty, and they have to save water.

Because there is no gravity, you don't use your muscles like you do on Earth. So astronauts have to exercise on special machines, to stop their muscles from wasting away.

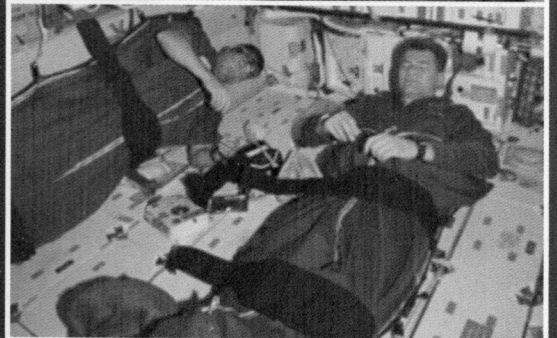

Purpose: _____

_____

_____

Register: _____

_____

_____

Content: _____

_____

_____

2 Imagine that you went on a virtual tour of a space craft and experienced what it is like to live the way astronauts do. Write an email to a friend and describe what you enjoyed most or least about the tour.

send	save	discard

To

Subject

_____

_____

_____

_____

_____

_____

_____

_____

_____

_____

_____

_____

_____

_____

_____

_____

_____

_____

3 Discuss your email and experiences with a group.

Look at and think about each of the *I can* statements.

Date: _____

1 Underline the subordinate clause in each sentence.

  a My brother, who loves stories about space, wants to be an astronaut.

  b I saw the movie, which you recommended, about the first moon landing.

  c My uncle, who loves science, explained what a tesseract is.

  d Astronauts eat food that is prepared on Earth.

  e Light from the Moon, which is closer to Earth than the Sun, takes 1¼ seconds to reach us.

  f Meg, who didn't understand, asked Mrs Whatsit to explain tesseracts to her.

2 Add a subordinate clause with commas to each sentence.

  a My uncle _____ is afraid of space travel.

  b The astronauts _____ walk around in space.

  c The packets _____ are put in a special bin.

  d The girl _____ wants to be an astronaut.

  e The book is about space travel _____

3 Read the dictionary entry and answer the questions.

---

universe (juːnɪvɜːʳs)

Word forms: plural **universes**

Countable noun

The universe is the whole of space and all the stars, planets, and other forms of matter and energy in it.

Einstein's equations showed the Universe to be expanding.

Early astronomers thought that our planet was the centre of the universe.

Synonyms: cosmos, space, creation, everything

---

  a What is the purpose of this type of writing?

  _____

  b What part of speech is the word 'universe'?

  _____

  c Use a synonym for 'universe' in a sentence of your own.

  _____

4 Write a dictionary definition for the word 'astronaut'. Include:

- the plural form of the word
- a definition
- an example sentence
- two synonyms.

_____

_____

_____

_____

5 **a** Work with a partner. Write five questions that you can use to interview someone to find out what they know about space travel. Start with the given words.

What _____

Why _____

How _____

When _____

Where _____

b Think about the answers to the questions and role-play your interview.

6 Compare the texts *A Wrinkle in Time* and *The speed of light*. Complete the chart that follows.

~ A Wrinkle in Time ~

"Nnow," Mrs Which said. "Arre wee rreaddy?"

"Where are we going?" Calvin asked.

"Wwee musstt ggo bbehindd thee sshaddow."

"But we will not do it all at once," Mrs Whatsit comforted them. "We will do it in short stages." She looked at Meg. "Now we will tesser, we will wrinkle again. Do you understand?"

"No," Meg said, flatly.

Mrs Whatsit sighed. "Explanations are not easy when they are about things for which your civilisation still has no words. Calvin talked about travelling at the speed of light. You understand that, little Meg?"

"Yes," Meg nodded.

"That, of course, is the impractical, long way round. We have learned to take short cuts wherever possible."

"Sort of like in Math?"

"Like in Math." Mrs Whatsit looked over at Mrs Who. "Take your skirt and show them."

"La experiencia es la madre de la ciencia. Spanish, my dears. Cervantes.

Experience is the mother of knowledge." Mrs Who took a portion of her white robe in her hands and held it tight.

"You see," Mrs Whatsit said, "if a very small insect were to move from the section of skirt in Mrs Who's right hand, to that in her left, it would be quite a long walk for him if he had to walk straight across."

Swiftly Mrs Who brought her hands, still holding the skirt, together.

"Now, you see," Mrs Whatsit said, "he would be there, without that long trip. That is how we travel."

Charles Wallace accepted this explanation serenely. Even Calvin did not seem perturbed.

"Oh dear," Meg sighed. "I guess I am a moron. I just don't get it."

"That is because you think of space only in three dimensions," Mrs Whatsit told her. "We travel in the fifth dimension. This is something you can understand Meg. Don't be afraid to try. Was your mother able to explain a tesseract to you?"

Meg sighed. "Just explain it to me."

From *A Wrinkle in Time*, by Madeleine L'Engle

The speed of light

Light travels through space (and air) at a speed of 299 000 km per second (186 000 miles per second). If you could travel at that speed, you could go more than seven times round the world in a second!

Scientists believe that nothing can travel faster than light. That is because there is not enough energy in the whole universe to make even the smallest thing reach that speed.

Light takes about 8¼ minutes to reach us from the Sun. So when you see the Sun, you are seeing it as it was about 8¼ minutes ago. Reflected light takes about 1¼ seconds to reach us from the Moon.

	A Wrinkle in Time	*The speed of light*
What is the text about?		
What is the type and style of text?	Fiction: fantasy/science fiction/narrative	
Is the language formal or informal?		
What is the purpose of the text?		
Does the text have facts and opinions?		

Look at and think about each of the *I can* statements.

Date: _____

1 Add a prefix to each word to make a word with the opposite meaning.

a direct _____

b afraid _____

c mobile _____

d known _____

e possible _____

f credible _____

g do _____

h accurate _____

2 Work with a partner to test your spelling. Say one of the opposite words you made in question 1 and let your partner spell it. Take turns.

3 Choose one verse from the poem *Gravity*, which you read as a group.

a Copy the verse here.

_____

_____

_____

_____

_____

_____

_____

_____

_____

_____

_____

b Make notes on the poem to show:

• which words you want to emphasise

• where you will change your voice

• what gestures or facial expressions you want to use as you perform.

c Read the verse aloud with expression.

4 Read the following lines from poems. Circle the rhyming words and underline the similes.

a Imagine all the trees come loose,

In orbit like a watery noose.

b Space is like the deepest sea

With not enough air for you and me.

c I wandered lonely as a cloud

That floats on high o'er vales and hills.

d Does your skin crinkle up

like a raisin in the sun?

5 Underline the metaphors in these lines from poems. Explain which two things are being compared in each metaphor.

a The broken circle of my family

gathers once a year for lunch.

_____

b You are a ray of sunshine in my life.

_____

c The stars are dancing through the sky tonight.

_____

d 'All the world's a stage, and all the men and women merely players.'
William Shakespeare

_____

6 Write a short poem about space. Include a simile or a metaphor in your poem.

_____

_____

_____

_____

_____

7 Make a list of some of the features of each type of text.

Information text	Story	Poem
• non-fiction	• _____	• _____
• _____	• _____	• _____
• _____	• _____	• _____
• _____	• _____	• _____

Look at and think about each of the _I can_ statements.

Date: _____

1 🎧 Audio 2 Listen to the news broadcast. Make notes about the main points of the news below.

_____

_____

_____

_____

_____

_____

2 Listen to the news broadcast again. Work in pairs and check the notes you have made. Are they accurate? Improve your notes.

3 Complete the chart. Write definitions of the words as they were used in the text you listened to.

Word	Part of speech	Definition	Word in a sentence
update			
switch			
stage			
unfold			

4   Scan this section of the news report for specific information to answer the questions.

> In international news, wildfires continue to blaze out of control in many areas of Canada. Firefighters have been working around the clock for more than two months to bring the blazes under control. With millions of hectares already burned this year, help is arriving from other countries in intensified efforts to control the blazes. Concern is now mounting over the poor air quality in many provinces of Canada. Climate change is probably responsible for the intensity of the wildfires this year.

a   Where are the wildfires burning?

_____

b   Give a synonym from the text for the word 'fire'.

_____

c   Explain what the expression 'around the clock' means.

_____

d   Why are these fires causing concern?

_____

e   What is the viewpoint of this reporter about the causes of the wildfires? Tick (✓) one answer.

☐   Climate change is the main cause of the wildfires.

☐   Climate change may be making the fires worse than before.

☐   Poor air quality is the main cause of the wildfires.

f   What is your viewpoint about wildfires? What can be done to prevent them?

_____

_____

5   Spell these words correctly.

a   sattelite _____   **b**   enviroment _____

c   immeditely _____   **d**   participasion _____

e   asistence _____   **f**   explotion _____

6 Choose the best modal verb, 'could', 'would' or 'should' to complete each sentence.

a You _____ always wear a life jacket when you are in a boat at sea.

b Climate change _____ be responsible for the intensity of the wildfires.

c I _____ hate to be alone out on a canoe.

d If we had been there, we _____ have witnessed the event first hand.

7 🎧 Listen to and then read the following eyewitness account of a volcano
Audio 3 eruption. This was originally written by a writer called Pliny the Younger, in Latin. He wrote the letter to an historian of the time Tacitus. It is about a volcano eruption in Italy in the year 79 CE, in which his uncle died.

Extracts from a letter: To Tacitus

My uncle was at that time with the fleet under his command at Misenum*. On the 24th of August, at about one in the afternoon, my mother desired him to observe a cloud which appeared of a very unusual size and shape.

A pine tree near Mount Vesuvius

…

A cloud, from which mountain was uncertain, at this distance (but it was found afterwards to come from Mount Vesuvius), was ascending, the appearance of which I cannot give you a more exact description of than by likening it to that of a pine tree, for it shot up to a great height in the form of a very tall trunk, which spread itself out at the top into a sort of branches.

…

As he was coming out of the house, he received a note from Rectina, the wife of Bassus, who was in the utmost alarm at the imminent danger which threatened her; for her villa lying at the foot of Mount Vesuvius, there was no way of escape but by sea; she earnestly entreated him therefore to come to her assistance.

…

He ordered the galleys to be put to sea, and went himself on board with an intention of assisting not only Rectina, but the several other towns which lay thickly strewn along that beautiful coast.

...

He was now so close to the mountain that the cinders, which grew thicker and hotter the nearer he approached, fell into the ships, together with pumice-stones, and black pieces of burning rock.

...

I will end here, only adding that I have faithfully related to you what I was either an eye-witness of myself or received immediately after the accident happened, and before there was time to vary the truth.

* Misenum: Ancient port town near Naples in Italy. Today it is called Miseno.

8 Answer these questions.

a Write three features that make this text a non-fiction recount.

_____

_____

_____

b When did Pliny's mother first notice the volcano?

_____

c Write a sentence that shows that the text is written in the first person.

_____

d To what does Pliny compare the cloud?

_____

e Give one fact in the account.

_____

f What fell on galley ships that sailed towards the volcano to rescue the inhabitants?

_____

Look at and think about each of the *I can* statements.

Date: _____

1 Rewrite the paragraph. Replace the words in bold with contractions.

My sister went out on her canoe yesterday morning. The sea was rough but she **did not** have her life jacket with her. She was very lucky that another canoeist saw her. She **could have** been in serious trouble if he **had not** come over to help her. She **should have** been more careful. **It is** often dangerous out at sea, especially if **there is** a strong current.

_____
_____
_____
_____
_____

2 Rewrite the sentences with apostrophes in the correct places.

a Theyre going to watch a movie tonight.

_____

b Alls well that ends well.

_____

c The mayors wife complained about the explosion.

_____

d I cant wait to hear my friends news.

_____

3 Punctuate the sentences correctly.

a do you believe the news I don't

_____

b whos coming with us to the sports centre

_____

c my brother doesnt work for the tv station any more

_____

d my dads family live in cairo

_____

4 Correct the errors in the sentences.

a You're sister is a surfer, is'nt she?

_____

b   Their going to give there reports this afternoon.

_____

5   Plan and write a short report about a sports event you have witnessed.
Your report should:

- have an interesting and informative opening sentence

- have short paragraphs

- include a quotation

- have formal but friendly language.

a   Plan your report.

```

```

b   Write your draft.

_____
_____
_____
_____
_____
_____
_____
_____
_____
_____

c   Evaluate your report with the help of a partner.

d   Improve your report and write it neatly in your notebook.

Look at and think
about each of the
I can statements.

Date: _____

1   Reread the article and answer the questions.

Can fame make the world a better place?

The organisation DoSomething.org has released its 7th annual 'Celebs Gone Good' list. The list ranks the top 20 celebs who use their fame (and fortune) to help others. For the third time in a row, singer Taylor Swift scoops the number one slot. Successful, smart and generous? That's the kind of girl we like!

Taylor Swift donated all of the money she earned from the sale of her single *Welcome to New York* to New York City Public Schools. So, if you bought this song, give yourself a high-five – because you've also done some good.

The actress Laverne Cox came in at number two. This ultracool feminist icon helped to get people talking about tolerating difference this year. Beyoncé slotted in 3rd for her #BeyGood campaign. Miley Cyrus follows closely behind for her work around the serious issue of youth homelessness. And rounding out the top 5 is yet another female star, Emma Watson, who blew the world away with a hard-hitting speech on gender equality at the UN. She also set up the #HeForShe campaign.

So … this year, it's all about girl power! Go girls – you rock.

a   How does this article attract and keep a reader's attention? Name two features of the article.

_____

_____

b   Write two informal expressions used in the article.

_____

_____

c   Write an example of a fact in the article.

_____

d   Write an example of an opinion in the article.

_____

2   Work in groups of three or four to read the article aloud.

a   Practise reading the text in an appropriate way, using:

- appropriate tone of voice
- gestures and facial expressions
- emphasis where you think it is necessary.

b   Present the article to another group.

3 Watch the news on television or listen to it on the radio. Use the form below to make notes about what you hear.

Notes about the news

Channel	
Time	
Headlines	
Main story	
Most interesting story	
Weather	

4 Use information you wrote down when you watched or listened to the news broadcast to make your own news presentation.

- Decide whether your broadcast will be formal or informal and use the appropriate language.

- Write your full presentation in your notebook or on a tablet to use in your presentation.

5 Use this checklist to evaluate each other's presentations.

- Did the news keep your attention?

- Was the language used formal or informal?

- Was the language appropriate for the content?

- Was the presentation clear and easy to understand?

- Did the presenter vary their tone of voice and expression?

- Did you enjoy the presentation?

Look at and think about each of the *I can* statements.

Date: _____

1 Complete the sentences with words from the box.

equator   wilderness   continent   deserts   savannahs   wildlife

a Africa has

_____,

_____

and rainforests.

b The _____ is an imaginary line that cuts across the middle of Africa.

c Have you visited any places on the _____ of Africa?

d In Africa you can see some of the greatest _____ in the world.

2 Scan the text and find the following.

a Synonyms for:

complicated _____

moves _____

varied _____

safe place _____

b Two words with three syllables each.

_____

_____

c A word made with each root word.

change _____

call _____

resemble _____

sad _____

d Contractions for these words:

It is _____

they are _____

THE OKAVANGO DELTA

Resembling an intricate maze with lagoons, swamps and islands – home to elephants, lions, leopards, buffaloes, giraffes, hippos, crocodiles, antelope and more than 450 species of birds …

This is the Okavango Delta in Botswana.

A UNESCO World Heritage site – and one of the wonders of Africa.

The water comes from the Okavango River – sometimes called 'the river that never reaches the sea'

Beginning in Angola and flowing inland through Namibia before it reaches Botswana, the river creates a diverse ecosystem in this otherwise desert land.

It's a sanctuary for wildlife - they're protected in game reserves.

In the mornings and evenings, elephants come down to the water to bathe, play and drink … crocodiles and hippos cruise in the water.

Sadly this ecosystem too is changing because of climate change and human activities …

e Words that are used to describe the following:

what hippos and crocodiles do in the water _____

what the delta looks like _____

3 Tick (✓) the sentences that describe the features of commentaries.

☐ They can be persuasive.

☐ They are non-fiction texts.

☐ They include personal opinions and viewpoints.

☐ They are fiction.

4 Work in pairs. Brainstorm some ideas to use in a short commentary about a country that interests you.

- Think about the vocabulary you will use in the commentary.
- Make notes in a list or a mind map.

5 Write a short commentary based on the some of the ideas you discussed.

_____

_____

_____

_____

_____

_____

_____

_____

6 Edit and improve the commentary.

7 Read your commentary to the class or record it and play the recording to the class.

Look at and think about each of the *I can* statements.

☐

Date: _____

1 Read the following text and answer the questions.

> Hans Ngoteya is a conservationist from Tanzania. He is also a professional photographer and film director. He is the founder of the Tanzania Wildlife Media Association, which promotes and educates people about the wildlife in Tanzania. He is also a co-founder of Ngoteya Wild, a Tanzanian wildlife and conservation company.
>
> He makes wildlife documentaries about sustainable wildlife practices. His aim is to help communities to coexist with wildlife, believing that this can be done through storytelling. He says that listening to talks on conservation is boring but 'moving images' get people involved, and that's why he decided to become a filmmaker.

a What is the purpose of this short text?

_____

b What information does the text not provide?

_____

c What other sources could you use to find out about this person?

_____

d What does Hans Ngoteya aim to do?

_____

e What, in his opinion, is a good way of achieving this?

_____

2 Write two paragraphs about a wildlife conservationist whom you know about from radio, television or magazines.

_____

_____

_____

_____

_____

_____

_____

_____

3   Read this extract from *The Greenhouse Effect*.

> The world is warming up a little more every year, and the warmer it gets, the more unpredictable the weather will be. So, why is this happening?
>
> Scientists think they know why. When we burn fuel – like oil, coal, or wood – we make a gas called carbon dioxide (CO_2). Today there is more CO_2 in the air than there has been for more than half a million years. Together with other gases, carbon dioxide acts like a greenhouse, trapping the heat from the Sun's rays in the atmosphere. Think of what would happen if you sat outside on a sunny day in a plastic raincoat. You'd get hotter and hotter.

a   Use the information from the text and the words in the box to label the diagram.

Sun's rays   atmosphere   trapped heat   carbon dioxide

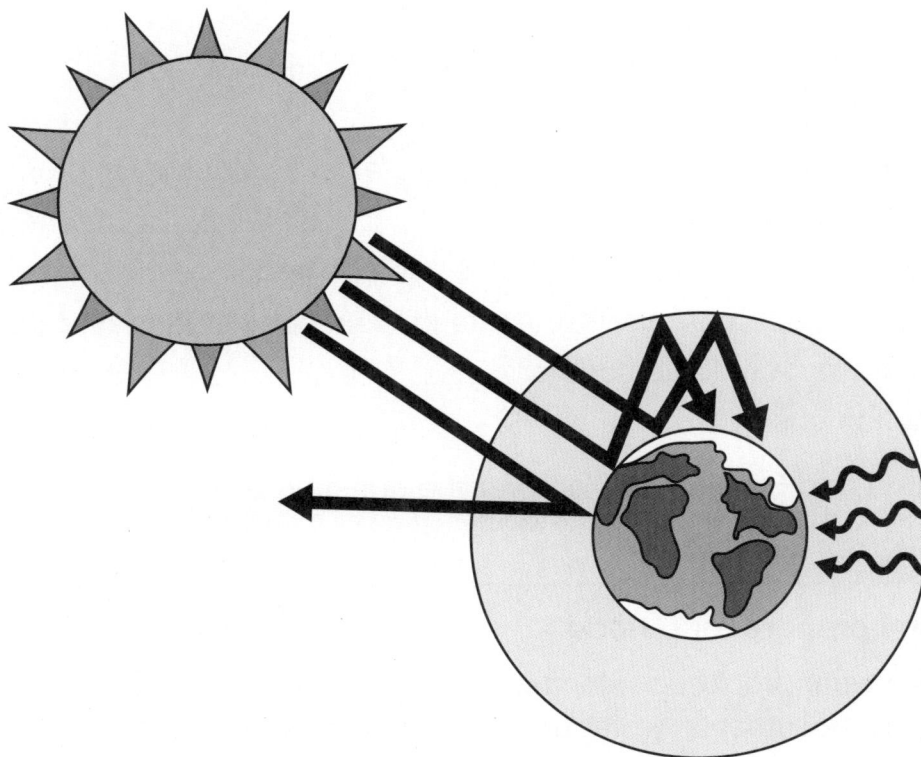

b   Explain what the greenhouse effect is to a partner, using your diagram.

c   Find the root word in the word **unpredictable** and then explain what **unpredictable** means.

_____

d   What is the Earth's atmosphere?

_____

e What is the meaning of **greenhouse** in this text? Tick (✓) one answer.

☐ a house that is painted green inside

☐ a structure that controls the temperature and climate in an outside area

☐ a house that uses solar power and rainwater instead of piped water and electricity

f How does the comparison with wearing a raincoat on a sunny day help us to understand the Greenhouse effect?

_____

4 Choose words from the box to complete the sentences about the features of information texts. You will not use all the words.

an index   fiction   a personal   non-fiction   diagrams
present   past   an impersonal   characters

Information texts are _____ texts. They give us information or

explanations. The texts are written in the _____ tense, usually

in _____ style. Features such as headings and

_____ are used to make the text easy to read and understand.

Some texts have a contents page or _____ to help the reader to

find information easily.

5 Read Texts A and B below and answer the questions.

Text A

How can I prepare for a flood?

- Pack a waterproof bag with medicines, a torch, first aid kit, change of clothes, personal documents, water and non-perishable foods.

- Keep your phone charged. Save emergency numbers on your mobile phone.

- Raise all electrical appliances, such as TV sets, fridges and stoves, off the ground and switch them off if water gets into the home.

- Prepare bags of sand to place around your home.

- Have an emergency family plan.

- Listen to the weather reports and follow advice from local authorities.

- Be ready to assist others who need help.

Text B

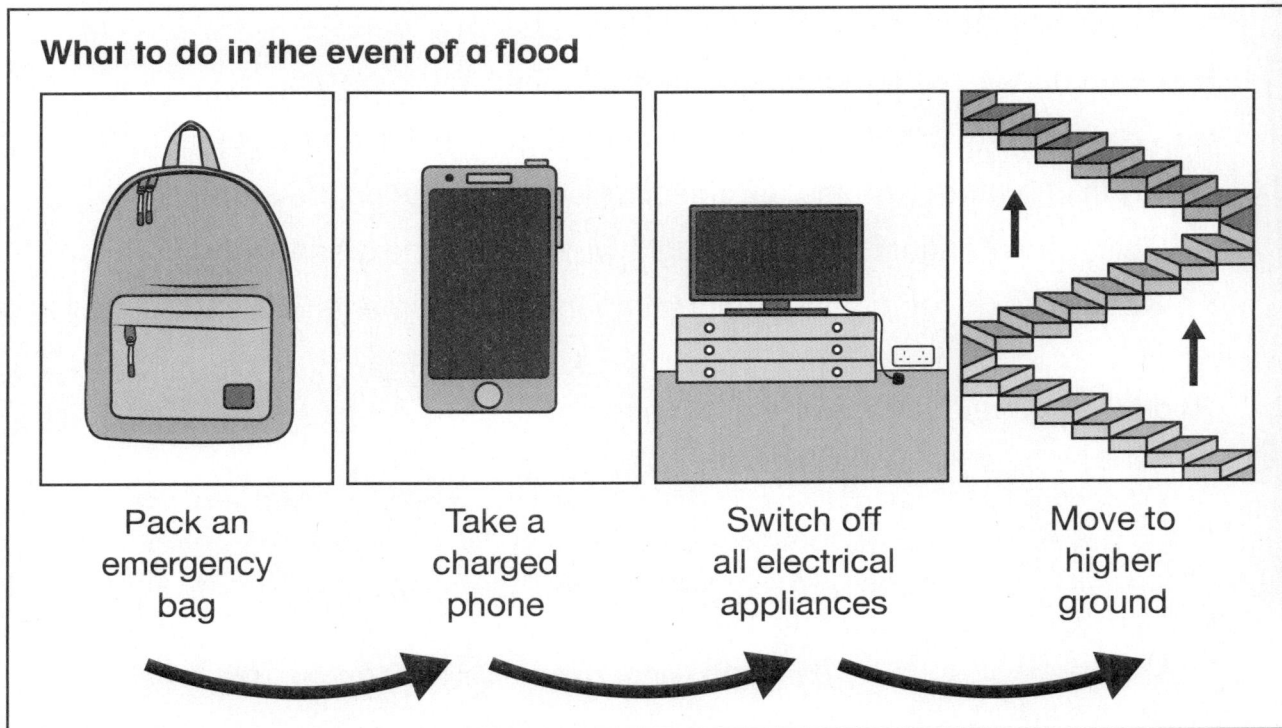

What to do in the event of a flood

Pack an emergency bag → Take a charged phone → Switch off all electrical appliances → Move to higher ground

a   What is the purpose of each text?

_____

b   Are the texts fiction or non-fiction?

_____

c   Which features make the texts easy to read?

_____

d   What should you pack in an emergency bag?

_____

e   What is 'higher ground'? Give an example based on where you live.

_____

f   Why do you think it is important to switch off all electrical appliances?

_____

6   Use the diagram to explain to a partner what to do if there is a flood near your home.

Look at and think about each of the *I can* statements.

Date: _____

1 Underline the correct word(s) to complete each sentence.

a The water crept (higher/high) until it reached my knees.

b Hurricanes used to happen (less/least) often in the past.

c When I am (oldest/older) I will build houses that don't break up in hurricanes.

d My little brother was the (afraidest/most afraid) during the storm.

e This is the (longest/longer) drought we have ever experienced.

f Keep your (most important/much important) documents in a special bag in case of emergencies.

2 Read the text and answer the questions.

> I'm Kathure. I don't understand climate change, but I know that the rivers have dried up and I have to walk a long way to collect water. I only have one meal a day, which I'm given at school. I feel so bad when I see my baby brother crying because he's hungry, and I can't do anything. I wish I could change this.
>
> When I grow up, I will plant crops that don't need much rain to grow. Then my family will have food.

a What type of text is this? Support your answer with a quote from the text.

_____

b Is the language formal or informal? Quote from the text to support your answer.

_____

c Why does Kathure have to walk a long way to fetch water every day?

_____

d How does Kathure feel about this?

_____

e In what way does Kathure hope to change things when she grows up?

_____

_____

3   Write a diary entry about climate change in the country where you live. Include the following information:

- How is the weather changing?

- How do you feel about this?

- What can you do to make a difference?

_____

_____

_____

_____

_____

_____

_____

_____

_____

_____

4   Write a poem or a short information text about climate change. Think about the features you need to use to write the text.

_____

_____

_____

_____

_____

_____

_____

_____

_____

_____

_____

_____

Look at and think about each of the *I can* statements.

Date: _____

1   Reading

Read the following text and then answer the questions.

In the Arctic Ecosystem

Arctic sea ice contains no soil, so no trees or grass grow there. But peer underneath, and you'll find a thick carpet of sea ice algae growing.

Algae is a plant-like living thing, that uses sunlight and **nutrients** to make food.

It's a rich source of food for tiny creatures such as krill, which are eaten by many **marine** animals, like fish, squid, clams, and even whales.

The smaller creatures are eaten by bigger fish, seals, whales and birds, which in turn are hunted by polar bears.

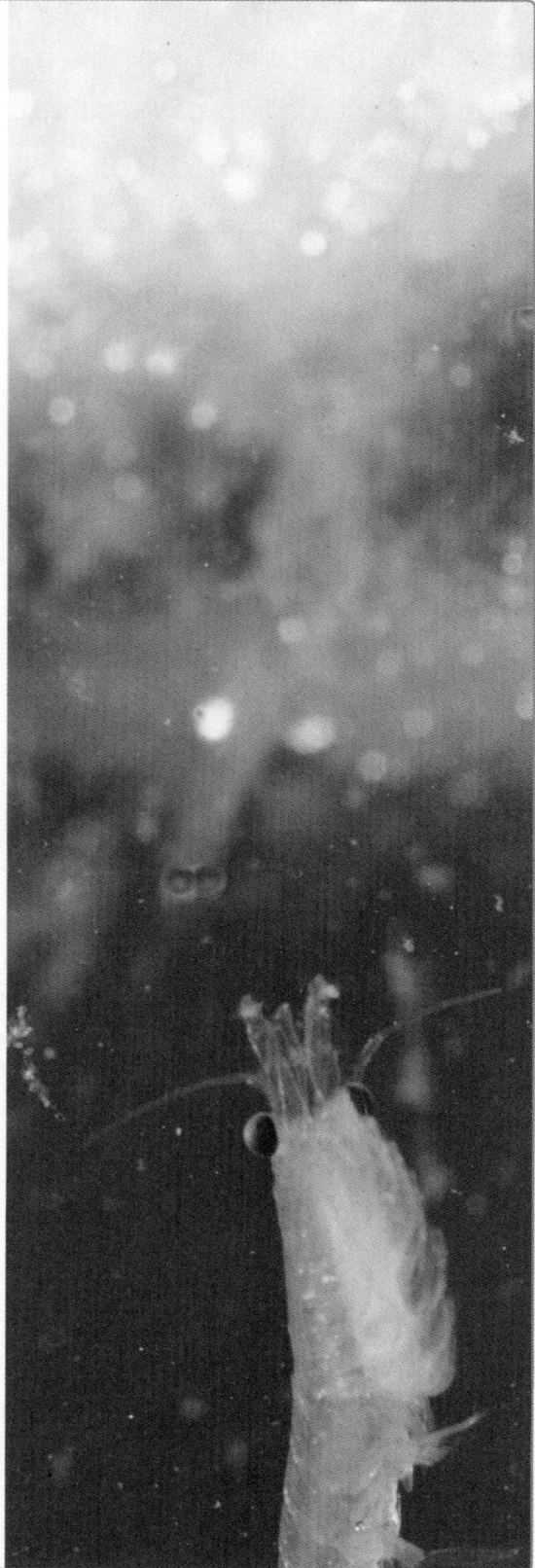

a What type of text is this?

_____

b Give a synonym for the word 'peer'.

_____

c What is a 'marine' animal?

_____

d Underline the main idea in this sentence.

Algae is a plant-like living thing, that uses sunlight and nutrients to make food.

e Explain the metaphor in the following phrase. What two things does it compare?

… a thick carpet of sea algae…

_____

_____

f What will happen if the ice melts? Quote from the text to support your answer.

_____

_____

_____

_____

_____

_____

2 Writing

a Complete each sentence by adding a suitable subordinate clause.

   i Krill, _____, feed on algae.

   ii Marine animals, _____, eat krill.

b Rewrite the sentences with suitable punctuation.

   i I would love to visit the arctic said susan

   _____

   ii A seals food is the smaller animals in the sea

   _____

c How would you write the sentence below in a formal text?

   Hey, did ya know? There's no soil under the Arctic Sea – nothing!

   _____

   _____

d Correct the following sentence.

   What are the most small living things in the ocean?

   _____

e Use a prefix to give this word the opposite meaning.

   living _____

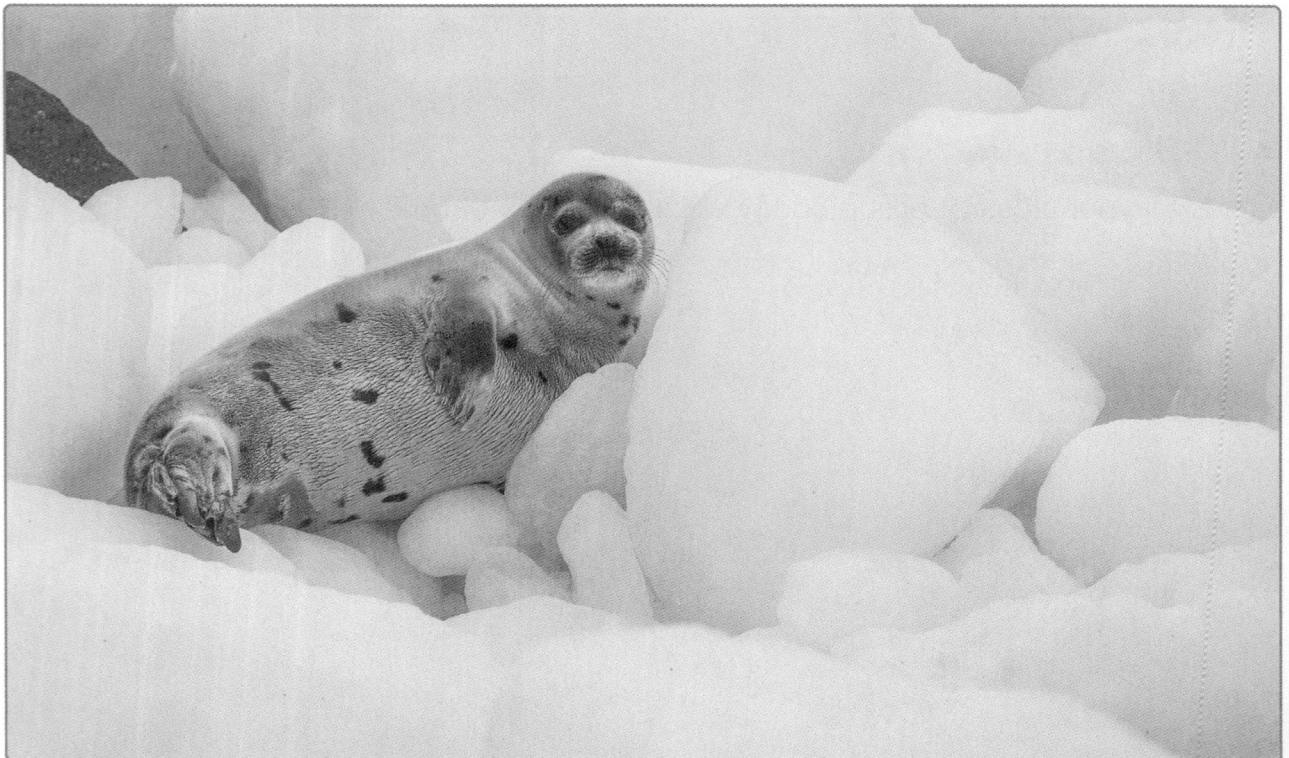

3   Writing

Write a paragraph based on the following notes about how the ice in the Arctic Sea is shrinking. Use language that is appropriate for an information text. Give the paragraph a heading.

Ice floats on the Arctic Sea at the North Pole.

The ice forms (freezes) in winter and then melts in summer.

Now, climate change – more ice melts in summer.

In 20–30 years' time – no more ice in summer.

Serious problem.

_____

_____

_____

_____

_____

_____

_____

_____

_____

_____

_____

_____

4   Speaking

Tell your class or group briefly what you know about climate change.

Give one example of how it affects the world.

Give one example of what we can do about climate change.

Look at and think about each of the *I can* statements.

Date: _____

Acknowledgements

Text acknowledgements

The publishers gratefully acknowledge the permission granted to reproduce the copyright material in this book. Every effort has been made to trace copyright holders and to obtain their permission for the use of copyright material. The publishers will gladly receive any information enabling them to rectify any error or omission at the first opportunity.

Cover illustration: *Alice in Wonderland* Reprinted by permission of HarperCollins*Publishers* Ltd © 2015 Emma Chichester Clark, illustrated by Emma Chichester Clarke; An extract on pp.12-13 from *Saffy's Angel* by Hilary McKay, first published by Hodder Children's Books in 2001, new edition 2021 by Macmillan Children's Books, an imprint of Pan Macmillan, copyright © Hilary McKay, 2001. Reproduced with the permission of Macmillan Publishers International Ltd; Margaret K. McElderry Books, an imprint of Simon & Schuster Children's Publishing Division; Extracts on pp.16, 57 from *Walk Two Moons* by Sharon Creech, first published by Macmillan Children's Books, an imprint of Pan Macmillan, 1994, copyright © Sharon Creech, 1994, Reproduced by permission of Macmillan Publishers International Limited and HarperCollins Publishers; The poem on p.26 "When the Teacher Isn't Looking" by Kenn Nesbitt, published in *When The Teacher isn't Looking: And Other Funny School Poems* by Kenn Nesbitt, Meadowbrook Press, copyright © 2005. Reproduced by permission of Running Press Kids, an imprint of Hachette Book Group, Inc.; An extract on p.34 adapted from *Rainbow Reading Level 5 – Move Your Body: Body Art* by Cheryl Minkley, copyright © Cambridge University Press, 2009. Reproduced with permission of Cambridge University Press through PLSclear; The poem on p.36 "A Bird Came Down the Walk" by Emily Dickinson, from The Poems of Emily Dickinson: Reading Edition, edited by Ralph W. Franklin, Cambridge, Mass.: The Belknap Press of Harvard University Press, copyright © 1998, 1999 by the President and Fellows of Harvard College. Copyright © 1951, 1955 by the President and Fellows of Harvard College. Copyright © renewed 1979, 1983 by the President and Fellows of Harvard College. Copyright © 1914, 1918, 1919, 1924, 1929, 1930, 1932, 1935, 1937, 1942 by Martha Dickinson Bianchi. Copyright © 1952, 1957, 1958, 1963, 1965 by Mary L. Hampson. Used by permission. All rights reserved; *Alice in Wonderland* Reprinted by permission of HarperCollins*Publishers* Ltd © 2015 Emma Chichester Clark, illustrated by Emma Chichester Clarke; An extract and image on pp.52–53 from *The Whale Rider* by Witi Ihimaera, Penguin, New Zealand, 2008, copyright © Witi Ihimaera. Reproduced with permission from Penguin Random House New Zealand; The poem on p.54 'Sea Fever' by John Masefield. Reproduced with permission from The Society of Authors as the literary Representatives of the Estate of John Masefield; *Stories in the Stars* Reprinted by permission of HarperCollins*Publishers* Ltd © 2022 Anita Ganeri, illustrated by Linh Nguyen; An extract on p.60 from 'Anansi and Horse' by Alexander Archibald, published in *Jamaica Anansi Stories* by Martha Warren Beckwith, 1924, used under the Creative Commons Attribution-ShareAlike License. Adapted by Karen Morrison in *Caribbean Comprehension: An integrated, skills based approach Book 5*, copyright © Hodder Education, 2014. Reproduced by permission of Hodder Education through PLSclear; Images on p.62 from "Anansi and Firefly go Hunting" from *Rainbow Reading Level 4 – Life and Living: Anansi and the Firefly* by Emma Attwell, copyright © Cambridge University Press, 2009. Reproduced with permission of Cambridge University Press through PLSclear; An extract on p.68 from *Rainbow Reading Level 5 – Space Workers* by Daphne Paizee, copyright © Cambridge University Press, 2009. Reproduced with permission of Cambridge University Press through PLSclear; and an extract on pp.71-72 from *A Wrinkle in Time* by Madeleine L'Engle, Penguin Books, copyright © Madeleine L'Engle, 1962, Crosswicks Ltd, 1967, and Penguin Random House LLC, 2012. Reproduced by permission of Aaron M. Priest Literary Agency; *Climate Change Heatwaves and Big Freezes* Reprinted by permission of HarperCollins*Publishers* Ltd © 2022 Mio Debnam.

In some instances we have been unable to trace the owners of copyright material, and we would appreciate any information that would enable us to do so.

Photo acknowledgements

The publishers gratefully acknowledge the permission granted to reproduce the copyright material in this book. Every effort has been made to trace copyright holders and to obtain their permission for the use of copyright material. The publishers will gladly receive any information enabling them to rectify any error or omission at the first opportunity.

P19 NAS CREATIVES/Shutterstock; p22 TORWAISTUDIO/Shutterstock; p28t Wirestock Creators/Shutterstock; p28b voy ager/Shutterstock; p34tl Delpixel/Shutterstock; p34tr Blend Images/Shutterstock; p34b Nadezhda Bolotina/Shutterstock; p36 cabuscaa/Shutterstock; p42 Everett Historical/Shutterstock; p54 Kostyantyn Ivanyshen/Shutterstock; p55 Repina Valeriya/Shutterstock; p58 Universal Images Group North America LLC/Alamy; p68t NASA; p68c NASA; p68b NASA; p68b DM7/Shutterstock; p76 Egoreichenkov Evgenii/Shutterstock; p78 imagoDens/Shutterstock; p82t Image Press Agency/Alamy; p82b REDAV/Shutterstock; p84 kavram/Shutterstock; p92 Flip Nicklin/Nature Picture Library; p93 Alexandr Medvedkov/Shutterstock; p94 CookiesForDevo/Shutterstock.